Stumped: How Trump Triumphed

The Open Secrets of Donald Trump's Gravity-Defying Political Domination and How You Can Use Them

J.M. Carpenter

DEDICATION

To my mentor in politics, H.S., for expanding my vision.

And to my parents for their love and support.

CONTENTS

Reactions against the previous regime benefitting those riding them, today's reaction as being against globalism, social justice warriors, and political correctness

How uncertainty benefits Trump in this particular race, despite people normally being risk-averse

Parallels to the nastiness and wildness of the 2016 election cycle, the potential Trump coalition, and the direction of the American political parties for the coming era

A history of presidential elections in light of the previous chapters, 2016 general election scenarios

Introduction: Defying Convention, Rethinking Assumptions

The first thing you need to realize about this book is this - you can't write a great story based primarily on logic and reason, you can't sell a product or service based primarily on logic and reason, and by extension, you won't get what you want in life based primarily on logic and reason. The mechanisms of influence do not arise from the neocortex, the logical part of the brain. If you're analyzing Donald Trump through a *strictly* logical lens, as most have done, nothing about his campaign makes sense.

The primary problem that the conventional wisdom in our political economy suffers from is that it puts too much faith in logic and reason and not enough in more esoteric, primal concerns that are more powerful movers of human action. Just saying this is controversial since it is essentially the foundation of Western thought since the Enlightenment. Yet, it seems clear that the Enlightenment thinkers of the 18th century, in the throes of their questioning of ancient tyrannies and superstitions, were *too* eager to throw the baby out with the bathwater when it came to understanding the nature of man.

The standard assumption we tend to have of man is as that of an almost exclusively rational creature, the *Homo economicus* of economic theory - an individual, atomized, self-interested agent acting in the pursuit of specific, utilitarian goals. This viewpoint bleeds over to politics as well, in which individual voters are often assumed to essentially be rational agents acting in pursuit of their own self-interest. It's a nice theory, uplifting even. It's nice to think of man as distinctly separate from all those dumb beasts we see around us. In its own way, faith lives on. Man is still created in the image of God, omniscient. It's also nice to think of ourselves as free from outside, perhaps unsavory influences, as enlightened beings ought to be.

Yet, the shortcomings of this viewpoint of man have become increasingly apparent in recent years. The *Homo economicus*, rational choice theory of man is incomplete at best, mostly wrong at worst. Faith, myths, stories, social orders, and hierarchies all matter. They are persuasive influences and more so than logic. It's why people are charismatic power players and it's why advertising and marketing works.

It's instinctive, emotive, visceral, and other "lower brain" factors that are the primary drivers of human decision-making, not rational, carefully examined choices based on perceived self-interest. Instead, logical, rational considerations usually come *after* the basic decision has already been made. This assuages doubt and lets the agent be at peace with what he or she has decided to do or believe, contrary to the conventional assumptions and wisdom in political economy. This includes human behavior in political choice.

All politicians know this to an extent. All play on emotions (notably fear), but Donald Trump is outcompeting them in those plays by leaps and bounds.

It was because of this viewpoint, honed within me over several years of widespread trial and error, that I called Trump's rise and continued march to victory earlier than most, though other figures like Scott Adams (creator of *Dilbert*, who's Trump Persuasion Series is excellent) and Mike Cernovich (Danger and Play, author of *Gorilla Mindset*) had me beat in terms of getting onboard the Trump Train first. I suppose that after he announced, my conventional political scientist's training took over and I believed that Trump would "flameout" during the summer, just as so many other unorthodox candidates had done before him. My only wish then was for him to do as much damage to the political and media establishment as he could.

That will be the only explicitly political "ought" stance found in this book. Any "oughts" from here on out are reflective of the reader, not me. **To put it clearly, this book is not endorsing Donald Trump.** This book instead is about an "is" or more generally a "how" – how Trump came to dominate.

After Trump made it through September of 2015, I realized that he was here to stay.[1] Once the "Summer of Trump" ended, my education took over from my schooling. I realized what Trump was doing and what school of thought he was operating out of. I know Trump's game because I use it, though obviously on a much smaller scale than him. The Trump campaign is all about entrepreneurship, marketing, sales, persuasion, thinking big, and bold self-assertion. When combined with an explosive electorate which is frustrated and ferociously angry with the established institutions, one that is clamoring for change, these elements served as the warm waters in the creation of a perfect political storm.

While Donald Trump does represent an overdue realignment in politics, his campaign is fascinating not just from a political standpoint, but because of the way he's using his skills as a marketer and salesman to gain so much traction. I study Trump as I want to improve my own game in the area, and ultimately, yours - because you can also pursue the same strategies to make your life better and get more of what you want.

In other words, this book is an intersection explaining how Trump – through boldness, marketing/sales, social dynamics, and conventional political science, stumped everyone and rose not only to frontrunner status, not only to the Republican nomination, but ultimately I believe, to the presidency. It's also a book about *you* and the life you can live when you recognize and implement Trump's playbook.

Scott Adams has suggested that a Trump win might force us to rethink our standard assumptions of human behavior and rationality.[2] I'm not so sure I agree with the prospect of such a huge change in thought based on one election, as the ideological assumption of rational actors is very deeply entrenched. This is itself indicative of the primary importance of stories and desires in determining what humans choose to ultimately believe and how they behave. However, the Trump campaign is a good test of two worldviews of human behavior. The first is the usually rational, as championed by the mainstream political, academic, and media establishment. The second is the often, if not usually irrational, championed by marketers, behavioral economists, and so on.

Because of the widely ingrained establishment consensus, we tend to believe that anything "irrational" is fundamentally bad. Yet, sometimes the irrational is necessary to ensure a degree of human happiness and flourishing. This is something that our "rational" assumptions have often tended to ignore, but that's a topic for another story.

***

Takeaways:

1. The major takeaway of this book is that people are not usually rational. Appealing to logic and reason will not usually move human beings to make decisions and won't bring you the power, riches, and prestige you desire. You must instead put your standard assumptions aside and learn to see human beings as primarily impulsive, visceral agents. This assumption being your new standard, you will now be able to build your

skills at influencing people.

2.   While this book will display the principles that Donald Trump uses to influence people and why they work, you'll ultimately need to apply them to your own personality. Each person will and must have his or her own way of using them. Authenticity, or rather, the perception of it, matters. Don't try to be someone you're not. Instead, use these principles as tools to help you in your quest to build the best version of yourself. They serve as capital for your construction project, but are not the project itself.

1. The Masculine Monster in the Beta Sea

Masculinity and dominance matter even more than normal in a nation starving for strong, decisive leadership. Into this atmosphere stepped Donald Trump, an unapologetic, masculine man who does what he wants and dominates the world around him. He signaled these things the moment he announced he was running for president, when he violated political orthodoxy and attacked numerous sacred cows.

Is this good or bad? It doesn't really matter. It put everyone on notice.

It's no secret that masculinity is in short supply these days. Testosterone and semen levels have dropped significantly in men in recent decades. More broadly, normal male behavior has been increasingly shamed, boys are falling behind in school, and society is becoming more and more androgynous. There were no such things as gender neutral bathrooms until a few short years ago. You'd be looked at as a crazy person for even suggesting the idea. The dominant leitmotif of maleness these days is the hipster wearing skinny jeans and thick-rimmed glasses. The much-maligned Pajama Boy from those Obamacare ads a few years ago (late 2013) was not an inaccurate depiction. Walk the streets of New York or any big city. Pajama Boys are everywhere.

This creeping effeminacy, or androgyny, is not limited to America's (or for that matter, the Western world's) youth. It's crept up into the leadership as well. One incident was particularly telling of the trend.

In mid 2014, a video was made public of President Obama working out in a gym in Poland. It was a rather pitiful sight. If it was deliberately leaked to make President Obama look tough, it achieved the opposite effect. The weights he chose, after much delay, were pitifully light. My father, who is now close to 70, would easily lift such weights…and with proper form, because the whole escapade was made worse by the fact that the Obama's form was terrible in doing exercises with those relatively light weights.

Go watch the Obama workout video on YouTube, keeping in mind that this is the current President of the United States, the man who, if push came to shove, would be tasked with annihilating the enemies of the nation. Can you honestly say that you would be intimidated by that?

No, you wouldn't be.

This, in a nutshell, is how the political establishment in both parties, as well as the media and academia, is popularly viewed today. These are the people that chart our course as a nation, even though they are seen by most, whether consciously or not, as pathetic and weak. The weightlifting is symbolic of that vacillating, indecisive weakness. They're perceived as pampered ivory tower theorists that live in their bubbles, whether they're in the halls of Congress and the think tanks of the Beltway, the TV studios and hedge funds of New York, or the halls of Harvard and Yale. In these echo chambers, they think they're smart and dominant, but if push came to shove, they'd all fold like a pair of 2's against a Full House. Despite the democratic zeitgeist that has arisen in the Western world since the Enlightenment, today's leaders and elite classes are arguably more out of touch with their own people than the kings and aristocrats of the past, who often took to the field of battle with them.

This is the sentiment amongst the public at large, even if the people you asked gave different reasons for it or called it in different ways. This is what they would be implying, knowingly or not.

When it comes to analyzing leadership, and what good leadership ought to be, an interesting standard to apply would be one based on the exploits of the 18th Dynasty Egyptian King Thutmose III, who faced a dilemma in the famous Megiddo Campaign of 1457 B.C. This might be called the "Thutmose test." Keep in mind that this test is not explicitly political, but rather one which analyzes leadership as a phenomenon.

There were three roads he could take to reach the city - a northern, a southern, and a narrow path through the nearby cliffs called the Aruna Pass, which was extremely dangerous. It was an ideal place to stage an ambush. If Thutmose's enemies caught him there, his army would have no room to maneuver and would be slaughtered. Yet, the pass was also the most convenient road, as it led straight to the city.

Despite the danger, Thutmose decided to move through the pass, banking on the assumption that his opponents would never suspect him to conduct such an audacious move. In this, he was right (this same phenomenon has also been true of the Trump campaign). However, that is not where the test gets its power.

Instead, it gets its power from the fact that the king decided to lead his men through the pass personally, taking their risk of an ambush and making it his own. Further, Thutmose gladly doubled his own risk by being front and center. He led the way, we are told by his scribe Tajenni, by his own footsteps. His bold gambit was successful. Stunning his foes, Thutmose went on to lead his men to a decisive victory.

In contrast to this, think of the leader that would wait for his men to march through the pass and get the all-clear before moving through it himself.

The former is a leader who will be seen as having demonstrated that he cares about his people and consequently will win their hearts and minds. The connection will instantly create charisma (see chapter 4). The latter, on the other hand, will be seen as a coward that uses his people as a means to an end.

If we had to describe good, inspiring leadership that raises morale, builds social bonds and trust (see chapter 5), and *causes human beings to act on that leader's behalf,* what Thutmose III did at Megiddo is a great example. When people see their king, decked out in royal regalia, marching and fighting with them, and taking double the risk, they'll instantly be drawn to him. That toughness and willingness to take on such risk inspires them to victory and to follow him into hell. Often it's been that the leaders who follow this style are the ones who win. That's because people instinctively seek out this kind of decisive, bold, and strong leadership. It's ingrained in our tribal nature. People respect strength and despise weakness, even if they aren't consciously aware of it.

Now, look at the state of the United States and the Western world in general (with Eastern Europe possibly exempted) and what do you see?

You see what was described at the beginning of this chapter! It's present in both the general public and in the leadership. For all our quaint notions of equality, the truth is that the Pajama Boy phenomenon is not something that inspires deep feelings of respect and devotion in others. Instead of being seen in the guise of Thutmose, most of our leaders are seen by the public as being Pajama Boys of one kind or another. Thus, they get no respect. A telling indication of this, and of how out of touch those in power are with these deeply human, tribal traits, is that the leadership in the ivory tower actually expected the electorate to respond warmly to Jeb Bush. Even when discounting the immense baggage that comes with the name - a terrible personal brand (see chapter 6) - Jeb Bush is just an archetypal example of the total lack of masculinity and fortitude perceived in the present leadership by the public, even if that public does not think of it in those words. Bush's run was made even worse by the fact that voters are sick of the Bush clan, political dynasties, and the kind of politics that the said dynasty espoused (see chapter 8). It was a dangerous gambit, and as soon as a viable alternative arose, the electorate took it.

Jeb Bush is a perfect example of the timid, weak, insecure man who cannot dominate, and so must submit to the stronger party. That party was Donald Trump, who shattered all the rules of political convention just because he could. If you haven't noticed by now, Donald Trump does and says what he wants solely because that's what he wants to do. He's an unapologetic character. You can either follow him or get out of his way, but you cannot control or bully him.

This attitude is the foundation of a masculine character, which now must be defined for the sake of clarity. My conception of masculinity is essentially Homeric. It's about dominating the world around you, doing things that are worthy of remembrance and celebration long after you die. This was known as *kleos* in the epic tradition. Louis XIV called it "true glory."[3] It's a lifestyle of doing, of action, of conquering obstacles. It instantly captivates attention and inspires others, especially if the person living that lifestyle connects with followers.

Unapologetic characters like Donald Trump are the best poised to act in this fashion.

This style of leadership, this trailblazing drive toward something greater, has not been witnessed for a very long time. Instead, the public perceives its leadership as being one of myopic, sniveling cowards that are bullied by their donors and "social justice warriors" (see chapter 9).

Yet, it was not always this way. The United States used to have very masculine leaders – not always, but often enough.

George Washington rode between the lines at Princeton while both sides were shooting at each other to rally his men.

Andrew Jackson fought duels and beat his would-be assassin with a cane, not to mention leading his men to victory in battle.

Abraham Lincoln was a strong man known as a railsplitter that balanced his strength with a stoic intellectual and political brilliance. His was a gentle, warm leadership.

Theodore Roosevelt overcame his asthma and frailness because he would not accept being a weakling. He went on to lead men into battle, box as president, and went up the dangerous Amazon River because he needed something to do. Oh, and he was shot in 1912 and still delivered a speech.

All of these men left their marks in history, dominating their respective eras.

George Washington held together a ragtag, desperate army and eventually defeated the most powerful military force in the world.

Andrew Jackson paid off the national debt; stood up to the establishment of his time, and ushered in a new age of American democracy.

Abraham Lincoln was brave enough to do what he needed to do to stop secession and then end slavery.

Theodore Roosevelt curbed the power of trusts to ensure a competitive marketplace and protected American workers and consumers from abuse.

Note that this is not an explicit endorsement of their policies per se. That's within the realm of reason/rationality, which is like trying to observe the universe in only the narrow band of visible light while missing the full spectrum of what's possible to measure. Rather, it's evidence that these men were able to impose their will on the world in the face of high opposition. Regardless of whether they were good or bad, they deeply inspired the people of their time to follow them, and we still remember them today.

We have not had this kind of larger-than-life, risk-taking, trailblazing leadership, the kind of leadership that takes the world by storm and brings forth a new, rejuvenated age for the betterment of the people, in a long time. Barack Obama was the hope of a great deal, but he was soon proven a failure on this front.

The people are yearning, craving for bold, decisive leadership to take the country in a new direction, even if they don't think they are. This burning desire for decisive, unapologetic, masculine leadership is made stronger by the fact that, for many years now, the majority of Americans have believed that the country is headed in the wrong direction, and not only that, but that America's best days are behind it. Such an atmosphere is the pressure cooker for a strong, masculine man to emerge on the scene to take control, provide direction, and stymie the fear (a very unpleasant emotion we wish to be rid of) that people are feeling.

The talking heads quickly predicted Trump's demise as soon as he announced and every time he pushed the envelope. "He's finally gone too far this time!" We would hear the same thing often several times a week. Far from his demise, Trump's outrages only made him stronger. This is a concept called antifragility, as laid out in Nassim Taleb's book *Antifragile: Things that Gain from Disorder*.[4] Being in an antifragile state is a good indicator of masculinity, as masculine men rise to meet and ultimately benefit from the challenges that face them – which is how they attain such status in the first place. Recall that in almost every culture throughout history, there was and is a rite of passage for a boy to become a man, meaning that manhood is associated with struggle and triumph. These rites of passage range from the relatively benign to the very vicious. For example, in our contemporary culture, the masculine rite of passage is usually for a boy to make enough money to strike out on his own (or risk becoming a "man-child stuck in his mother's basement"), whereas in Ancient Sparta, the custom was for a young Spartiate on the verge of being considered a full member of society to kill an indentured servant, called a helot, and not get caught.

In essence, masculinity is something that must be *earned*. It is not given. Donald Trump earned his in a political context by being, in the public's mind, brave enough to challenge the status quo in a way not seen in decades. He partially did this by knocking down sacred cows that the politico-media-academic-donor establishment class (referred to as "the ivory tower" or the "optimates" throughout this book) use to make itself look good, which is simply status-seeking behavior. In fact, this status-seeking is needy and vacillating, and therefore not masculine. It is not dominant, but supplicating. This behavior has been hammered out more concretely by James Bartholomew at *The Spectator*. It's a concept he calls "virtue signaling." A person is virtue signaling when he or she advocates a position not because of its innate correctness or truthfulness, but because advocating it is a quick, cheap way to gain social status and recognition. This has often been associated with the left wing, where people jump onboard bandwagons to squawk about how good they are as people by showing how much they hate right wing parties, publications, or those who run afoul of politically correct orthodoxy. This allows them to get a quick social high by telling others how "not racist," open, and accepting they are. Yet, when push comes to shove in doing something that *actually* requires virtue through effort, such as charity work, the same people take no heed of the call, as effort is largely alien to them.[5]

In actuality, by virtue signaling, they're attempting to establish themselves as members of a "cool" in-group in contrast to a lame or hated out-group (a powerful social phenomenon which will be examined in subsequent chapters).

Though it's usually associated with leftists, the traditional Republican establishment and the conservative movement from which it gets its finances and intellectual foundation, the "right wing" of the ivory tower, virtue signals just as much as the left wing. A great example during the early days of the Trump campaign was the brouhaha over John McCain "not being a war hero." The ivory tower was quick to react, saying that it would be the death knell of Donald Trump's campaign. Bill Kristol of the *Weekly Standard* was quick to call "peak Trump."[6] Instead, Trump's poll numbers *rose*, and the ivory tower was aghast. It couldn't explain it and was quick to take McCain's defense, virtue signaling by talking about how brave he was and how awful Donald Trump was.

The truth of what this virtue signaling really was wasn't lost on the electorate, and it quite frankly did not care about John McCain being "a war hero," especially given the fact that McCain is seen by many as a "RINO" (Republican in Name Only).

Secretly, people just love that Donald Trump is refusing to kowtow to establishment politics, that he does not let these unspoken, self-imposed political rules define him, that he refuses to be bullied by special interests or self-proclaimed victim groups. Instead, he's his own character, which is a major facet of his draw. Donald Trump makes his own reality, he does not let others make it for him (you'll see *how* he does this in chapters two and three).

Every time someone in the ivory tower has challenged him, including his opponents, Trump has not only won, he's become more popular. He has grown progressively stronger and the ivory tower progressively weaker.

People are attracted to those they perceive to be winners; those who exude power, strength of character and mind, a spirit of perseverance, indomitability, and unbridled self-confidence. They're attracted to those who they believe can lead them into battle and to victory. They're attracted even more to those who they believe will fight alongside them in their cause and share in the danger. Donald Trump conveys all of that. You wouldn't think that he's almost 70 by watching him.

Donald Trump is the most masculine man in the race.[7] Not only that, he's the most masculine man we've seen in politics in a long time. This is a huge part of why he's winning. Boldness is always respected, timidity never.[8] Bold, self-confident leaders and masculine men thus have a decided edge when it comes to winning elections against less sure, less masculine opponents. If we look at the history of American presidential contests (and we will in chapter 12), we can test this hypothesis – that bold, charismatic leaders that conquer obstacles and inspire confidence in the electorate by doing so, win elections. Meanwhile, timid, uncool candidates tend to lose.

It's well-known among political scientists that in American elections (in general, not just presidential), the man with the stronger, more chiseled jawline has tended to win. It's also known that the guy that is cooler, the "guy you'd want to have a beer with," as it's often called in this field, has tended to win, as seen notably in recent elections like in 2012, when Barack Obama beat Mitt Romney, and in 2004, when George W. Bush beat John Kerry. Both Romney and Kerry were often seen and portrayed by their opponents as being out of touch stiffs. The phenomenon goes back further. One *very* interesting comparison is the career of Andrew Jackson, who many have cited as a precedent for Donald Trump. Andrew Jackson was wildly popular with the general public both for his accomplishments and his conquering attitude.

Andrew Jackson, who would certainly have won a contemporary "beer test," catapulted to the presidency by beating John Quincy Adams essentially twice, because he won the popular and electoral votes but lost in the House of Representatives in 1824. Adams was seen as a pouty, entitled establishment character that denied the will of the people in 1824 and was a member of a political dynasty. In a wave of populism inspired by Jackson's character, the perception of corruption in Washington, and by bringing out people to vote who had never voted before (and many indeed could not previously), Andrew Jackson crushed John Quincy Adams in 1828 and realigned American politics.

The "beer test" actually may be more accurately seen as a test of how much confidence prospective leaders inspire in their followers – how well they do on the Thutmose test. This was especially seen in the case of Jackson. It's in a sense, not "having a beer," but whether *people want to follow* that leader, to admire him, to go into battle with him. How much confidence does he instill? How much does he inspire his followers to help him get them to the promised land?

Whatever anyone wants to say about Donald Trump, to his followers, he provides those feelings and projects that image – that you want to be around him, that he makes you better, that you want him leading you through hardship. This is one reason why people are more tolerant of his gaffes and his outrages that would have killed anyone else – because no one else provides that image and feeling of decisive leadership. Donald Trump does. His critics simply cannot find an alternative leader that inspires the same feelings that Trump does in his followers. Hence, they have been unable to rally against such a man.

***

Takeaways:

1. People respect boldness and hate timidity. If you are seen as being hesitant by those you wish to influence for one second, they will lose respect for you, as it will create doubt in them. Thus you will be far more unlikely to influence your prospect.

2. When in a leadership position, do not ask subordinates to do anything you wouldn't do yourself. Instead, lead from the front conspicuously.

3. When embarking on any endeavor, you should believe in your heart of hearts that it's absolutely the right thing to do. Once you arrive at such a decision after careful consideration, take the path without apology or second-guesses. To reinforce your decision, take repeated small actions to kill procrastination (your ultimate enemy) and cultivate the belief in the rightness of what you're doing in your subconscious mind, even if you have to lie to yourself at first should your conscious mind doubt your path. The actions you take will overcome the doubtful voice in your head, because you'll be forced to focus all your attention on your actions instead of talking to yourself and creating objections. Taking action will activate the attention center of your brain, the reticular activating system, and make you highly motivated to complete those actions, because this part of the brain hates incompleteness.[9] Above all, do not be afraid to fail. Small failures *will* make you naturally more confident in the future. Once you have made up your mind, spend less time thinking and more time acting. To quote Louis XIV: "There are often troublesome occasions which may cause you to hesitate in making a decision, but once you do, and think you have seen the best course, you must take it."[10] Should you cultivate this attitude and communicate it with authenticity, others will follow, because you will be perceived as strong and bold.

4. Do not think of your obstacles as problems, but challenges and opportunities.[11] Train yourself to make this a habit.

5. Don't be afraid to tear down sacred cows. Just having the guts to do so will alone win you some level of respect and prepare you to implement the lessons of the next chapter.

6. If you project the image of a bold, unapologetic character and leader, people will be more tolerant of your mistakes, because your confidence in yourself will obviously be visibly high to them. If you are so confident in yourself, why should your prospects and followers not be confident in you?

2. Dominate that Space!

Trump's grand plan stems from the foundation of his influence skills, namely, that he is the only bold, unapologetically self-confident leader and the only masculine man in the race. Furthermore, he is the only person of that kind we've seen in such a prominent position in a long time.[12]

As already laid out, my conception of masculinity is Homeric. That is, winning great glory for yourself and conquering any obstacles on your way to that glory, where you will be remembered and celebrated long after you're dead. This requires effort, self-reflection, perseverance, dedication, and ultimately…dominance.

If masculinity had to be described with just one word, it would be that – domination.

Masculinity, conquering obstacles, winning *kleos*, is fundamentally rooted in domination. To win, you must dominate the world around you. If you do not dominate the world around you, you will not achieve true glory. You will be mediocre. You will not be respected. You will not be living life on your own terms.

For those who disagree, let's take this to the most primal level possible, the origin of human behavior through the evolution in our brains over so many millions of years. Human mating behavior is essentially animalistic. Our attraction triggers, like most other behaviors that we can observe in the realm of choice, do not arise from the "thinking" part of our brain, the neocortex, but the instinctual, reactive parts.

When pondering this, ask yourself who will be more attractive to women? Furthermore, who will be more likely to amass a following of admirers (male or female)? Will it be an unapologetic man who makes his own choices and dominates the world around him or a man who only does what others tell him?

That masculinity is rooted in domination doesn't mean you go out and beat people with clubs. There are many ways to dominate and gain glory. The recently-deceased Antonin Scalia was a great example. Scalia was so influential and his thoughts so dominant in his chosen field that he will influence future attorneys and judges for generations to come, perhaps for as long as the republic exists.

That is dominance. That is masculinity. Scalia stood up for what he believed in, even when it was unpopular, and did his best to dominate his field. He wound up doing a fine job.

Donald Trump is doing the same thing in politics now. As he is the only masculine man in the race, he is dominating his opponents, and dominance is the foundation of the Trump campaign's grand plan, namely **domination of space.**

Spatial dominance is one of the sacred truths of military science. Your goal is ultimately to dominate space and to deny it to your enemy. It's a maxim in hand to hand combat and it's seen in the use of area denial weapons from landmines to iron spikes designed to stop horses, such as at Julius Caesar's siege of Alesia in 52 B.C.

There are two games which simulate warfare that strategists of all kinds have been playing for millennia: Chess and Go. The game of Go in particular is based around dominating space. Your goal is to acquire as much territory as possible and deny it to your opponent, hemming him in. Go can be seen as the strategic and operational simulation of war, while Chess can be seen as the tactical simulation (destroying your opponent's army to capture the space he holds).

Out of all the candidates running, Donald Trump is the only one who seems to understand the concept of spatial dominance (even if he himself may not put it in those terms) and he uses it at all three levels: tactical, operational, and strategic.

Let's look at some of Donald Trump's most infamous quips during the campaign:

> When Mexico sends its people, they're not sending their best. They're not sending you. They're not sending you. They're sending people that have lots of problems, and they're bringing those problems with us. They're bringing drugs, they're bringing crime, they're rapists, and some, I assume, are good people.
>
> – June 16th, 2015, campaign announcement speech.

> When I came out there, you know, what am I doing? I'm not getting paid for this. I go out there, and you know I didn't know there would

be 24 million people, but I knew it was going to be a big crowd because I get big crowds, I get ratings. They call me the "ratings machine." So I have, you know she…she gets out and she starts asking me all sorts of ridiculous questions and you know, you could see there was blood coming out of her eyes, blood coming out of her…wherever…but she was…in my opinion she was off-base. And by the way, not in my opinion, in the opinion of hundreds of thousands of people on Twitter because it has been a brutal day – in one way a great day for Fox, in another way, in the Twitter-sphere, it's been very bad, because she's been very badly criticized. She's a lightweight; I couldn't care less about her. In fact, you're competing against her and I'm doing your show.

– August 7th, 2015, on *CNN Tonight* with Don Lemon.

There were actually two key points of Trump's campaign war plan embedded in this quote. Do you know what the other one was? You'll see in the fifth chapter.

Now you're talking about sneaky, dirty, underhanded people that want to kill our civilians. They want to go after our civilians. They want to kill not only our civilians, all over the world, and it's gonna be stopped. It's gonna be stopped. Somebody criticized me the other day because they asked me what I'd do, and I said…I'm gonna bomb the shit out of them! It's true! I don't care! I don't care! They've gotta be stopped! They've gotta be stopped, and they should have been stopped a long time ago. So in Paris the other night, a horrible thing, and then all of a sudden we attack and France attacks all these different sites that they have, right? Why didn't they do this a year ago, two years ago? Why didn't they do it? Why did they wait? They always wait for a tragedy to happen! They're never forward, they're always waiting! So you say "oh wow, these are training centers, camps," by the way, what did they attack? They attacked the oil! Remember I've been saying for two years…attack the oil! Everybody said "oh Trump with the oil!" But I said more than attack it, I said attack it, take it, and keep it, that's what I said! So now they're attacking the oil and a couple of the people really said 'you know that was Trump's idea.' I've been saying this for two years, because a big source of their wealth is the oil.

– November 17th, 2015, campaign speech.

Donald J. Trump is calling for a total and complete shutdown…of Muslims entering the United States…until our country's representatives can figure out what the hell is going on!

– December 7th, 2015, campaign speech.

Where most saw outrage of some kind, such as bigotry or vulgarity, I saw plays to dominate space. If you're having a reaction to any of these "outrages," whether that be positive or negative, it means he's gotten to you. He's dominating conversational space as well as the space in your own mind. *You're thinking of him and not his opponents.*

Ever hear the maxim that it's better to be hated than ignored? It's true. If you're ignored, you may as well not exist. It's certainly true in politics, where name recognition is one of the surest and most reliable indicators of victory. Indeed, one of the advantages Trump had in the campaign from day one, and why he proved so much more resilient than other unorthodox candidates, was because the American public had known him for decades. In sales and marketing, familiar brands will often be the preferential choices of a consumer compared to brands he is less familiar with, even if the other brand may be cheaper and/or higher quality – a sure way of knowing that rationality models do not always make sense, that they are missing something important. The same instinct is also at play in politics. The familiar is comforting. The unknown is a cause for anxiety. You'll see all the details of this in the sixth chapter.

Those who are hated by some, perhaps even most, but loved by others, have often been pivotal figures in history that have brought lasting change. Julius Caesar and Napoleon Bonaparte are two such examples that do indeed seem to share many character traits with Donald Trump. Crucial American figures that we've discussed in the last chapter shared this polarizing characteristic also, such as Theodore Roosevelt and Andrew Jackson.

Donald Trump is certainly a polarizing figure. You either despise him or you adore him. What you don't do is ignore him. His opponents on the other hand are usually ignored. As such, they do not exist and therefore cannot win.

A great anecdote of Donald Trump's mastery of spatial dominance (in politics, that being the communicational space, the ways of getting your message out and establishing yourself in the public mind on your own terms) is when he bought the domain name "jebbush.com." Once secured, Trump had it redirect to his own campaign website. In one fell swoop, a crucial territory was denied to Jeb Bush and his own name was used against him as a way to promote his fiercest opponent.

Military scholars usually consider warfare as having applications on three distinct levels. As mentioned above, Trump's playbook covers all three. This chapter is a broad overview of how Trump dominates space in all three dimensions of warfare, in this case, political warfare. The rest of the book will drill down much more deeply into each dimension. The three traditional levels of warfare are the following:

Tactical: The level of individual field actions in close contact with the enemy, such as a battle.

Operational: The level of the campaign for an extended duration of time, say, for a year, to achieve a specific purpose.

Strategic: The level of the conflict as a whole, based around goals for a successful cessation of hostilities that meets the objectives of the respective warring party.

Note that the conduct of warfare at the lower levels is meant to serve in pursuit of the goals of the higher levels. Tactical considerations should not be used to dictate operations, and operational considerations should not be used to dictate strategy.

In the days prior to the first Super Tuesday on March 1st, both Marco Rubio and Ted Cruz attempted to out-Trump Trump by hurling character and reputational attacks (the effectiveness of which as a whole will be examined in the next chapter). This was very different from the kind of campaigns they were running before, with Ted Cruz running on the frame that he was the only consistent conservative and Marco Rubio running on the frame of preparing America for the 21st century within the traditional globalist, GOP establishment context.

Yet, by doing this, they allowed tactical considerations to dictate operations and strategy. They bought into Trump's own frame (the key concept examined in the next chapter). For this reason, I predicted it would have no impact, or even a negative impact, and Trump would continue to cruise to the nomination. I was so confident in this that I archived my tweet at the time of initial composition. You can view it here: http://archive.is/U5XeR

Ted Cruz and Marco Rubio applied this concept incorrectly. Donald Trump has usually, with only recent severe deviations (see below), done the opposite. He is using all of these dimensions properly in pursuit of his end-goal: being elected.

Tactical:

This can be drilled down to the level of individual issues and the way Donald Trump interacts with his opponents.

In political science, there is something known as the Overton Window, which is defined as the boundary of acceptable public discourse on certain issues. For example, in 1880, segregation was firmly within the bounds of the Overton Window. Integration was not, and no one running on such a platform would be able to get elected. Over a century later, it is the total opposite.

In traditional politics, politicians say only what they think they can get away with and no more. This, you may have surmised from the first chapter, is a fundamentally antithetical standpoint to masculinity, as it is weak. It allows space to be denied to you on your own account in order to seek approval, and unsurprisingly, the candidates in presidential electoral history that have dominated the most space on the key issues of the day have almost always won.

Trump, on the other hand, through repetition and bombast, has instead forced the Overton Window to follow him. Whatever the issue is, he's set the limits, and others therefore have to play by his rules. This allows him to dominate the issue and the conversation around it. Therefore, when the issue comes up, the public will associate it with one man and one man only: Donald Trump. Agree with him or not, the only game in town on the issue is Trump's. All of his seemingly outrageous statements served this purpose. He then further reinforces these statements and keeps the Overton Window where he wants it to be by taking advantage of the mental trick that presuppositions play on the human brain. He often says phrases like "a lot of really smart people think that I'm right" or "everyone agrees that illegal immigration is a big, big problem now because of me, and the all talk, no action politicians I'm running against won't be able to solve it." In addition to creating social proof (see chapter 5), this leads the brain on a linguistic path that almost forces it to accept the statement as being true.[13]

As Trump has dominated the conversational space of his issues, his opponents can only be reactive, not proactive, giving them no space to operate in. They are hemmed in on the political Go board. At best, they look like they're only following Trump's lead. At worst, their attempts look like impotent, flailing efforts to manufacture outrage in order to stop him in a decidedly anti-establishment election cycle. Whatever option, *he* wins. This keeps the initiative in his hands.

Indeed, Trump himself has mentioned this in his *The Art of the Deal* when discussing the concept of having leverage over others. Yet, he also mentions that leverage isn't always clear-cut, and it sometimes requires creativity or even a gross misrepresentation of the truth to acquire:

> When the board of Holiday Inns was considering whether to enter into a partnership with me in Atlantic City, they were attracted to my site because they believed my construction was farther along than that of any other potential partner. In reality, I wasn't that far along, but I did everything I could, short of going to work at the site myself, to assure them that my casino was practically finished. My leverage came from confirming an impression they were already predisposed to believe.[14]

Trump is certainly imaginative. When he seems to come out of left field with his tough stances on issues or his attacks on opponents, he is finding ways to create leverage to dominate space, ways which will force opponents to be reactive and play in his territory. This denies them the ability to be proactive and carve out their own.

And as for getting the word out, as he calls it, on issues, Trump operates in much the same bombastic way:

> The final key to the way I promote is bravado. I play to people's fantasies. People may not always think big themselves, but they can still get very excited by those who do. That's why a little hyperbole never hurts. People want to believe that something is the biggest and greatest and the most spectacular.
>
> I call it truthful hyperbole. It's an innocent form of exaggeration – and a very effective form of promotion.[15]

In essence, Trump asks for so much more than he really wants to both secure leverage and get attention to the issue or the exchange. He can then maneuver the negotiations into getting what he was really after all along.

On the level of tactics, it's Trump's calling card, and he's done it exceedingly well.

In this context, it's easy to make a prediction on Trump's "deportation force" plan. It's hyperbole. If he were president, he would not deport millions of people. He will however, use the threat as leverage to pass certain immigration reforms that he desires, probably including the wall.

Where other politicians only operate in what they think is the safe territory of the Overton Window, Trump scouts ahead, takes the nearby high ground, and secures a commanding position to dominate the battle. This is proper tactics.

Operational:

This is best exemplified in how Trump handles the media itself. To pursue strategic aims, he needs to dominate the conversational space for the long term, and he does this with methods of communication old and new.

Regarding traditional mass media – television, radio, newspapers, and so on, Donald Trump has said flatly that he uses these outlets for free publicity because he knows they need him to increase their own ratings. This is another method behind his bombast. The media loves controversy, and in the age of outrage, this is especially so. Donald Trump has simply made the media dependant on him. From that point, he is able to dominate the conversational space of the election cycle. He blatantly says it in *Crippled America*.[16] This allows Donald Trump to not only save money on costly ads, but generate social proof, a far more effective form of advertising than writing an ad.

Donald Trump is also his own media mogul. He has millions of followers on his social media outlets like Facebook, Twitter, and Instagram. As such, he's able to bypass the traditional gatekeepers and take himself directly to the people. He's said numerous times that his Twitter is like owning the *New York Times* without the losses. No other candidate has anywhere near this independent/social media presence at the grassroots, and this forces them in some respects to play ball with the traditional media – begging for airtime or print space with often hostile journalists, all the while Trump gets to take his own, unedited, raw message out to a greater number of people.

This combination is why Donald Trump has "sucked all the oxygen" out of everyone else's campaigns, even including his Democratic opponents who he has not directly sparred with yet (as of the time of this writing). He dominates the communications space. As such, Donald Trump is the dominant figure on the Go board. His opponents are hemmed in both on the issues and in their operations to get their messages out to the people. As they have less media presence, they have fewer resources to mount an effective counterattack.

The traditional media is also losing money as internet communications skyrocket. The 2016 election cycle, perhaps the first with a truly decentralized media apparatus that has reached full maturity, has managed to blunt the power of SuperPACs and the infamous *Citizens United* decision, as seen with the rise of Donald Trump and Bernie Sanders and the fall, or rather, the long dying, of Jeb Bush, who raised more money for a SuperPAC than anyone in history prior to his announcement (which is why he announced so late, after everyone knew he was running anyway). This democratization of communications and their effect on the election cycle has allowed for the bypassing of the ivory tower apparatus of big money and big media and is a key theme in chapter 7.

As this media superstructure changes and grows more diffuse, the traditional way of dominating operational space will also grow more diffuse. Negative television attack ads based on SuperPAC money will lose influence. Marketing savvy based on decentralized communications will increase in importance. The new political centers of influence may not be mass media and donor networks, but those who can work internet infrastructure and are masters at content marketing.

Donald Trump is a content marketing master, and he is using both old and new forms of media to occupy all conversational space. His opponents are so hemmed in that they cannot get any of their messages out. This is why all the negative attacks in the traditional media and from donor networks have not worked on Trump – because no one knows who anyone else is (relatively speaking, of course). On the other hand, familiarity completes sales. Every factor works in Trump's favor.

Strategic:

The goal of a political campaign is to get elected, to win more votes than your competitors. To do this, you need to create an electoral coalition and bring it out to the polls. This is something that Mitt Romney's tactical and operational maneuvers couldn't do. In fact, he and his efforts were so impotent, he dominated such little space, that he couldn't even energize his own base, and millions that could have made that election far more competitive stayed home.

There are many who lambaste Donald Trump as not being a "real conservative." And they are right. It's quite clear that Donald Trump, for all his bluster, differs with the conservative movement's efforts of the past few decades in numerous important ways.

What they don't get is that the conservative movement simply doesn't dominate enough space among the electorate to build winning coalitions anymore, and arguably hasn't since 1992.

However, by casting off the conservative straitjacket and by forging his own bold, new path in right wing politics, Donald Trump is using his tactical and operational maneuvers to put together a winning coalition at the strategic level.

There are indications that Donald Trump has wide crossover appeal. In the primaries thus far, Republican turnout has been at record levels while Democratic turnout has declined. In his victories in New Hampshire, South Carolina, and Nevada, Donald Trump won with every major demographic – rich, poor, young, old, college educated, non-college educated, white, non-white, and so on. He's been bringing out voters that haven't voted before, so-called "lost voters" that haven't voted in a very long time, voters that have switched parties, and possibly even a large percentage of Democrats in the general election.

The possible Trump electoral coalition will be discussed more in depth in the eleventh chapter.

Dominating the space of issues and the airwaves all serve this one goal – to dominate electoral space to put together enough votes for winning the election. Thus far, it all appears to be working for Donald Trump.

In 2004, Steven Pressfield wrote an excellent book, *The Virtues of War*, a fictionalized first-person account of Alexander the Great during his campaigns. When dictating the proper conduct of warfare to his impressionable 18-year-old nephew who had just received his commission, Alexander demands:

> When deliberating, think in campaigns and not in battles; in wars and not campaigns; in ultimate conquest and not wars.[17]

Sun Tzu famously advises his reader to know what the victory conditions are before embarking on hostilities, writing that victorious warriors win first and then go to war, while warning that the losing warriors fight first and then seek victory.

The latter describes most politicians, including Trump's opponents. They have ad hoc plans, especially in light of Trump's hemming them in, as seen with Marco Rubio's efforts prior to March 1st. He attempted to beat Trump in a battle of wits and failed. Trump, on the other hand, has (usually) stuck to his grand plan throughout his campaign. For convenience, it can be summed up as such:

Tactical level: Dominate winning, existential, visceral issues by moving the Overton Window with repeated bombast and then defend that ground against the reactive attempts of opponents.

Operational level: Dominate all conversational space by generating media attention, even if negative, and amass a huge following at rallies and on social media to bypass the gatekeepers.

Strategic level: Leverage the issues and the message and direct them at a winning electoral coalition to increase voter turnout and deny traditional power blocs to opponents.

Throughout this campaign, it hasn't been "let me tell you about my ideas" for the other candidates, but rather "let me tell you how I can beat Donald Trump." That is the power of viewing the world as a Go board and taking action to dominate space.

Yet, not even Donald Trump follows this with 100% devotion. As March was winding down, he let an attack against his wife, Melania, by a Cruz SuperPAC in Utah get to him. The attack in question involved a nude photo that was taken of Melania during her modeling career. While this attack would be effective amongst Mormons in Utah, most of the electorate would not regard it with much care. Instead of taking this into account, Donald Trump let this tactical development dictate operations and strategy, when he responded with a counterattack, in the form of a retweet, against Cruz's own wife. This counterattack was quickly followed up by a gaffe on abortion with Chris Matthews, where Trump responded that women should be punished for having an abortion should it be made illegal. While this made logical sense, the emotional resonance of the issue matters far more. Trump was thus thrown off his usual; marketer's game and was taken down to the realm of logic at his expense. Because of his response to these tactical developments, the narrative that Donald Trump was "anti-woman" emerged more forcefully than ever before. This occurred at the same time that he could have been dominating space on a signature, visceral issue of his, terrorism, in the form of the Brussels bombings on March 22nd. He was thus, for the first time, fighting a fight not of his own choosing. Those two developments were the biggest mistakes of Trump's campaign, and they did make a difference in Wisconsin, where he lost decisively.

Donald Trump thus represents both the blueprint of sticking to your grand plans and the warnings of what could potentially happen should you allow yourself to be deviated from them by lesser developments.

***

Takeaways:

1. View the wider world in some ways as a Go board. In every avenue of life there will be spaces to occupy. You must formulate a grand plan to occupy that space. Not every field is as cutthroat and competitive as politics, but you will always have competitors. Figure out your end strategic goal/s and then formulate operational and tactical plans accordingly.

2. Tactics should never dictate operations. Operations should never dictate strategy. Each lower level is meant to serve in pursuit of higher-level goals. Do not ever expend resources on a lower level engagement that is lost if it will negatively impact a higher level of your grand plan.

3. You must be eminently familiar with all modern and emerging avenues of communication and how you can occupy space within those realms. Communication is how humans intermediate thought about everything beyond the immediate senses. Failure to understand the means of communications will mean you cannot dominate space to engage in outreach and influencing efforts to achieve your ends. You will be ignored or dominated by someone else, as Jeb Bush was by Donald Trump.

4. The Overton Window is not something that exists simply in politics. Whatever the case in your own life, do not allow yourself to be confined within arbitrary boundaries of what is considered acceptable. You do not need to "go full Trump," but you should take the boundaries to where you want them to go, eking out your own space, rather than cowering in a small entrenchment on the field. Understand that your fears are illusionary. Take the repeat small actions advised in the last chapter in your quest to dominate space and they will disappear.

5. When moving the Overton Window and imposing yourself firmly in the minds of your prospects, use the power of presuppositions to reinforce the space you dominate. This leads your audience to believe what you want it to believe. Ask presuppositional questions such as "how will you handle the debt crisis my opponents will bring?" Additionally, make statements such as "of course, it's very clear that my product or service is the easiest way for you to increase conversions by 50%."[18]

6. When carving out your own space, find creative ways to secure leverage in negotiations or discourse. Research your opposition religiously and find their desires and fears, then be as imaginative as it takes to display that you can move the appropriate levers related to them. Use their desperate desires to lead them on or create a fear regarding your ability to upset their plans, even if your methods seem remote to you. Their emotions will get the better of them as they won't be thinking clearly. Instead, their pre-existing biases will be speaking loudest to them. Your job in creating leverage from thin air is to play to these. Make sure you collect as much information as possible, including on their dirty laundry. Train yourself to seek and ask for more. Be a bit bombastic. Hem your opponents in with your demands.

7. Advertising works, but free advertising is both more effective at influencing people and better for your pocketbook. Generate attention by eking out your own territory. Don't be afraid to be a bit controversial (but in the appropriate measure based on your station in life, of course). By being somewhat bombastic, by speaking in a somewhat hyperbolic fashion, you will generate attention and word of mouth, which in turn will increase your exposure and ultimate conversion rate. As Trump remarked, people are drawn to spectacles. Be one in your own way.

8. What demographics do you want to influence? Which do you need to attain your strategic ends? Leverage all your efforts to dominating the space in their minds and getting them to act in the way that serves your goal. This is the purpose behind all of your efforts. Efforts that do not further serve this purpose are wasted.

3. Frame, Attack, Counterattack

This chapter turns to perhaps the thing Donald Trump is most famous for – his constant attacks and the seemingly impervious deflector shield surrounding him. "Teflon Don," as he's been called because of his seemingly bizarre invincibility to gaffes, is that way in large part thanks to two things – his unshakeable frame and his constantly being on the offensive.

Steven Pressfield's *The Virtues of War* illustrates the concept and Donald Trump's standard operating procedure:

> Always attack. Even in defense, attack. The attacking arm possesses the initiative and thus commands the action. To attack makes men brave; to defend makes them timorous. If I learn that an officer of mine has assumed a defensive posture in the field, that officer will never hold command under me again.[19]

Nothing better describes the Trump campaign than this. Donald Trump dominates space. He does not surrender it. He almost always refuses to apologize or backtrack to his opponents or the media because doing so would be surrendering space. The conversation would shift from him and his own terms to the terms of some other entity. The Go board would change, and given Trump's frame of being a winner, a shattering of that invincibility would have devastating consequences.

Like all politicians, Donald Trump attacks the reputation of his opponents. However, his methods are far different than those of others, who usually attack the reputation of their opponents based on their policies, track records and perhaps their donors to establish the frame of a conflict of interest. Donald Trump does do this of course, and with added effect based on his outsider status in this year of the outsider.

The deadliest weapons in Trump's arsenal, however, are personal attacks. He bulldozes the very fiber of his opponents' beings. He also concentrates those forces on one decisive threat until that threat is neutralized.[20] Trump's campaign began with Jeb Bush as his most serious rival and the heavily-favored frontrunner from the start. Indeed, many pundits immediately predicted that the general election would be Jeb Bush vs. Hillary Clinton and that we should all just forget about it. Knowing this, Donald Trump conducted a massive offensive against Jeb Bush from the get-go.

He attacked Bush in the traditional way, questioning his ability to be independent of the substantial donor network he had put together for his SuperPAC and his ability to negotiate with Vladimir Putin. When on the latter attack, Trump would repeatedly ask, humorously, almost tauntingly – "who do you want negotiating with Putin, Trump or Bush?" in a tone of condescension. Trump also attacked Jeb Bush as being weak on illegal immigration because of his Mexican wife.

While the latter attack was certainly personal, the former two also have embedded personal attacks in them as well. The typical politician attacks a track record, usually implying dishonesty or incompetence, which, in political terms are fairly innocuous traits. They're simply expected as part of the nature of the political game. Trump on the other hand, implied character flaws far deeper. In the first, he implied corruption. With Putin, Trump implied that Jeb Bush was essentially a wimp that would get run over. This was a roundabout attack on Bush's masculinity while Trump was touting his own. The last attack dealt with immigration and Jeb Bush's connection to a foreign country which Trump repeatedly claims is "killing us on trade and at the border." This essentially implied that Bush was loyal to another tribe above his own – treason.

Dirty? Undoubtedly. Effective? Absolutely. Trump quickly overtook Jeb Bush in the polls, but that still did not quite solve the problem. Jeb Bush was no longer the clear frontrunner, but he was still hanging in there and presumably would once again overtake Trump after the long-awaited "flameout."

Trump then came up with a new attack, the effectiveness of which was so devastating that perhaps even he himself did not realize how much power it would ultimately hold. He called Jeb Bush "low energy" as the summer of 2015 was nearing its conclusion, which was the time when the conventional wisdom said that Trump would crater. Instead, exactly the opposite occurred. Trump's share of the vote in September jumped towards 30% while Jeb Bush would hover in single digits for the rest of his campaign. From then on, Jeb Bush was associated with being "low energy."

To add one final insult to injury, Trump continued to frame Jeb Bush as a wimp in this infamous exchange in a debate in December:

Jeb Bush: This is a tough business to run for president.

Donald Trump (interrupting, making a face): Oh you're a tough guy, Jeb, I know.

Jeb Bush (over audience laughter): And we need to have a leader that is principled. You're never gonna be President of the United States by insulting your way to the presidency.

Donald Trump (at the same time): Real tough. You're real tough, Jeb. Oh yeah (as Jeb finishes)? Well let's see, I'm at 42 and you're at 3, so so far, I'm doing better. So far, I'm doing better (audience cheers)! You know you started off over here Jeb (pointing at the podium next to him), you're moving further and further, pretty soon you're gonna be off the end (of the stage).

– CNN Debate, December 15th, 2015

Immature perhaps, but devastatingly effective. With all of these attacks, Donald Trump not only impugned Jeb Bush's reputation, loyalty, masculinity, and character, but he anchored them all to something sensual and easily visible. *It is* plausible to think of Jeb Bush as being "low energy" or wimpy based on his mannerisms, so the attacks stuck like tar, and he was trapped in that frame ever since.[21]

Before Super Tuesday, Donald Trump did the same thing to Marco Rubio, calling him "little Marco." As seen with Jeb Bush, this attack is anchored in visible reality when observing Marco Rubio's mannerisms. His late attacks on Trump *did* seem juvenile. *He does* often seem like a nervous wreck. His youth and inexperience have been used against him by others, and "little Marco" cuts into this as well. "Little Marco" is also devastatingly dismissive, setting Trump up as the masculine, alpha male swatting away a yapping, annoying dog.

Since this attack occurred so late in the game, when Rubio was already floundering, its overall effectiveness on the Go or Chess board is a bit unclear, but if it had occurred earlier, it would have likely achieved similar results to the attacks on Jeb Bush. In the elections after Super Tuesday, Rubio tanked to fourth place behind even John Kasich in some states, such as Mississippi.

Both of these case studies display that Donald Trump is always on the offensive. When attacked, he does not retreat (and thus surrender space), he counterattacks. Doing so allows him to maintain his standing, his frame, while unsettling the frames of others. Jeb Bush and Marco Rubio could not maintain their own frames and reframe to counterattack Donald Trump. By the time they came up with any answer at all, it was much later and far too late.

Frame is at the heart of the tactical level of the grand plan. It's from this that Donald Trump attacks, receives the efforts of his opponents, and then counterattacks. It's something again alluded to in *The Virtues of War*.

> Don't punch; counterpunch. The purpose of an initial evolution - a feint or draw - is to provoke the enemy into committing himself prematurely. Once he moves, we countermove.[22]

Donald Trump has often described himself as a "counter-puncher," even if this may not always be the case. Yet his "counter-puncher" strategy is joined at the hip with his bombast, because there is yet another element to it. The bombast simply gets his opponents to react, allowing him to control the frame of the discussion and dominate the space. By feinting against his opponents or being as offensive as he possibly can – and it doesn't take much in today's age of social media hysteria – his opponents surrender the initiative to him while he retains his own frame. He then puts his opponents in a frame of his own (whether that is as a low-energy person or as a little boy), taking territory on the board while maintaining a strong line against any counterattack. The result is that Trump gets to dominate his issues while his opponents don't have space to maneuver, only to attack him, and then to inevitably get beaten back in a counterattack. Trump's opponents are then not defined by their issues, but by what he makes of them.

Frame can be a bit difficult to describe sometimes, but it's something we all know exists subconsciously. It explains to a very large degree the phenomenon of social hierarchies. Remember back when you were in school and the coolest guy always seemed to be dominant, while you or somebody else were goaded into dancing to his tune? That's frame.

The guy at the top of the social ladder is the guy with the strongest frame. The hierarchy can be seen as one of frames. The one who imposes his frame on others is the superior one and the one who has another's frame imposed on him is the one that is inferior. The one who can impose no frame is lowest on the ladder. The guy who cannot have a frame imposed upon him is at the top.

You can of course choose not to play this game by absconding from the ladder, but by doing so, you're essentially an omega exile with no friends, or indeed, any social relations.

Frame is just as prevalent in politics as it is in high school. Issues, attacks, and counterattacks are put in the context of specific frames. Whether Marco Rubio is a "choke artist" or whether Donald Trump is a conman depends in large part on the public's perception, and the public will more easily think of Ted Cruz as a liar, say, if he appears to backtrack or be deferential around the frame set by his opponent accusing him of such shenanigans. An apology or backtrack, a surrendering of frame, is a tacit admission of guilt in the public's mind.

This was why, in the days before Super Tuesday, Donald Trump infamously refused to outright disavow David Duke on CNN after having done it the previous Friday (and note that he did it in such a way as to be dismissive of the claim, rather than actually acknowledging it) during a press conference in which Chris Christie endorsed him. Donald Trump knew that disavowing it again, under such an inquisitive atmosphere as CNN's *State of the Union*, would be a loss of frame.

Did Donald Trump maintain his frame in the best way that time? Probably not (unless he was using it as yet another ploy to dominate space, which is possible since it definitely drew all attention away from his competitors, Ted Cruz and Marco Rubio, going into Super Tuesday), but I can say that as someone who has studied and applied this concept for years, Donald Trump has the strongest frame I have ever seen.

There's been a meme going around for months that "you can't stump the Trump." This relates fundamentally to his frame. Donald Trump imposes his frame on others. He does not let others impose their frames on him. Thus, he cannot be stumped.

Donald Trump never backs down, apologizes, or backtracks, no matter the pressure, even if he's wrong. He deflects, he digresses, he shifts the conversation, he counterattacks.

Perhaps the most famous example of this occurred in Trump's exchange with Megyn Kelly in the first Republican debate on August 6th, 2015:

> Megyn Kelly: Mr. Trump, one of the things people love about you is you speak your mind and you don't use a politician's filter. However, that is not without its downsides, in particular, when it comes to women. You've called women you don't like "fat pigs," "dogs,"

"slobs," and "disgusting animals." Your Twitter account…

Donald Trump (interrupting): Only Rosie O'Donnell.

Audience laughter.

Megyn Kelly: No it wasn't. Your Twitter account…

Donald Trump (to the audience): Thank you.

Megyn Kelly: For the record, it was well beyond Rosie O'Donnell.

Donald Trump: Yes, I'm sure it was.

Megyn Kelly: Your Twitter account has several disparaging comments about women's looks. You once told a contestant on *Celebrity Apprentice* it would be a pretty picture to see her on her knees. Does that sound to you like the temperament of a man we should elect as president, and how will you answer the charge from Hillary Clinton, who is likely to be the Democratic nominee, that you are part of the war on women?

Donald Trump: I think the big problem this country has is being politically correct. I've been challenged many times by so many people and frankly I don't have time for total political correctness and to be honest with you, this country doesn't have time either. This country is in serious trouble. We don't win anymore. We lose to China. We lose to Mexico both in trade and at the border. We lose to everybody! And frankly, what I say, and oftentimes it's fun, it's kidding, we have a good time, what I say is what I say. And honestly Megyn, if you don't like it, I'm sorry. I've been very nice to you although I could probably maybe not be based on the way you have treated me, but I wouldn't do that. But you know what? We need strength, we need energy, we need quickness, and we need brain in this country to turn it around, that I can tell you, right now.

– Fox News debate, August 6th, 2015.

Note his response. He did not affirm or deny the question. To do so would be to acknowledge its premise and therefore operate within its frame. That would be a defensive tactic, not an offensive one that dominates space. Instead, Trump shifted the frame onto something else – first Rosie O'Donnell, a figure likely to be hated by the Republican Party's base, then to a polemic against political correctness, which also scored him points with the base, then to an attack on Kelly, questioning her fairness, then to a selling point for him – how he'd bring the country back from defeat, all within one counterattack!

Donald Trump's exchanges with Jeb Bush in the primary season's debates are also world-famous:

> Dana Bash: Governor Bush, Mr. Trump has suggested that your views on immigration are influenced by your Mexican-born wife. He's said that "if my wife were from Mexico, I think I would have a soft spot for people from Mexico." Did Mr. Trump go too far in invoking your wife?
>
> Jeb Bush: He did. He did. You're proud of your family just as I am. To subject my wife to the middle of a raucous political conversation was completely inappropriate and I hope you apologize for that, Donald.
>
> Donald Trump: Well I have to tell you, I hear phenomenal things, I hear your wife is a lovely woman.
>
> Jeb Bush (interrupting): She is. She's fantastic.
>
> Donald Trump: I don't know her and this is a total mischaracterization of what I said.
>
> Jeb Bush (continuing): She is absolutely the love of my life and she's right here, why don't you apologize to her right now?
>
> Donald Trump: No, I won't do that because I said nothing wrong, but I do hear she's a lovely woman.
>
> – CNN debate, September 16th, 2015

Trump maintained his frame by refusing to apologize to Bush's wife. In the first few debates, Jeb Bush's frame was *very* weak, the weakest of all the major candidates. It was so weak that even the ivory tower pundits couldn't claim that he did well. He lost much of what was left of his support throughout the autumn of 2015 in part because of his weak frame in the debates during that period. The status of "establishment favorite" in the race steadily shifted from him to Marco Rubio, who he attempted to hammer for his poor attendance record in the Senate, but wound up losing to Rubio's counterattack.

Jeb Bush's frame did get better as 2015 drew to a close and winter came, but by that point it was too late. Nevertheless, though Jeb Bush improved his frame, it was still but a speck on Donald Trump's:

> Jeb Bush: But what Donald Trump did…was use eminent domain to try to take the property of an elderly woman on the strip in Atlantic City. That is not public purpose! That is downright wrong! And here's the problem with that! The problem was it was to tear down (repeats three times) the house.

> Donald Trump (interrupting): Jeb wants to be a tough guy; he wants to be a tough guy tonight. I didn't take the property…

> Jeb Bush: You tried! And you lost in court.

> Donald Trump: I didn't take the property. The woman ultimately didn't want to do that, I walked away…

> Jeb Bush (interrupting): That is not true, and the simple fact is…to turn this into a limousine parking lot for his casinos is not a public use, and in Florida…what we did, we made that impossible, as part of our constitution. That's the better approach. That is the conservative approach.

> Donald Trump: Let me just, you know he wants be a tough guy…a lot of times, you'll have…and it doesn't work very well with him. A lot of times…

> Jeb Bush (interrupting): How tough is it to take away property from an elderly woman?

> Donald Trump: Let me talk. Quiet (putting finger to his lips). A lot of times… (audience boos) …that's all of his donors and special interests out there. So…that's what it is! And by the way, let me just tell you, we needed tickets, you can't get them. You know who has the tickets to the television audience? Donors, special interests, the people that are putting up the money (booing continues). That's who it is! The RNC told us…we have all donors in the audience and the reason they're not loving me, the reason they're not loving me (booing continues)…excuse me! The reason they're not loving me is I

STUMPED: HOW TRUMP TRIUMPHED

don't want their money. I'm gonna do the right thing for the American public. I don't want their money, I don't need their money, and I'm the only one up here that can say that.

– ABC debate, February 6th, 2016

In addition to demeaning Bush's toughness and masculinity, Trump shifted attention away from an unpopular opinion (eminent domain). He reframed the audience's boos and the issue on hand as him doing the right thing for the American people by being independent of the donor class! He not only imposed his frame on Jeb Bush, he did so on *the audience*.

In any of these instances, if Trump apologized, backtracked, or reconsidered, he would be letting someone else impose frame. Unlike other politicians, Trump doesn't do this. Instead of vacillating, instead of doing only what he thinks he can get away with and no more, Trump bulldozes anything he sees as an obstacle and he forces his opponents to respond, thus getting them to buy into his frame.

When seemingly caught in a bind, he just counterattacks. When attacked by Jeb Bush or anyone else, he reframes it as them trying to get their energy up, please their donors, or improve their poll numbers.

Now what happens? People think of Jeb Bush as being low energy. They think of John Kasich and others as being low in the polls (a doubly effective reframe since it shows a lack of social proof, see chapter 5). They think of Ben Carson as being run by his SuperPAC. His opponents now react, affirm Trump's frame, and make themselves look worse.

The attack changes the conversation. Donald Trump *never* assumes a defensive posture in the field.

Ted Cruz has the second-strongest frame in this election cycle. Because of this as well as his being decent at other strategies found in this book, he has proven the most resilient of Trump's competitors. Like Trump, he does not backtrack or apologize and has some bombast of his own. It's a good frame, but still nowhere near as good as Trump's. In fact, Trump threw Ted Cruz off his frame numerous times.

First, Trump brought up the issue of Ted Cruz's eligibility to run for President of the United States under the Constitution's "natural born citizen" clause. After that, Cruz had to spend time clearing up doubts instead of being on his message when he began to grow his support. Cruz surrendered space, Trump gained it. Trump also sowed doubt in Cruz's supporters, and if a buyer has doubt, the sale will not occur.

Cruz then tried to attack Trump via the avenue of "New York values." In other words, he was questioning whether Trump was a "real conservative," a tactic designed to sow doubt in Trump's own supporters. Trump instead reframed, as seen most notably in the last debate before the Iowa caucuses in January 2016:

> Ted Cruz: I think most people know exactly what New York values are.
>
> Maria Bartiromo: I am from New York, I don't!
>
> Ted Cruz: You're from New York, so you might not (audience laughter). But I promise you in the state of South Carolina...they do. And listen, there are many, many wonderful working men and women in the state of New York, but everyone understands that the values in New York City are socially liberal or pro-abortion or pro-gay marriage...and I guess I can frame it another way. Not a lot of conservatives come out of Manhattan; I'm just saying (audience laughter).
>
> Donald Trump: Conservatives actually do come out of Manhattan, including William F. Buckley and others, just so you understand. New York is a great place, it's got great people. It's got loving people, wonderful people. When the World Trade Center came down, I saw something that no place on Earth could have handled more beautifully, more humanely than New York (audience applause). You had two 110 story buildings come crashing down, I saw them come down, and we saw more death and even the smell of death. Nobody understood it, and it was with us for months, the smell, the air, and we rebuilt downtown Manhattan, and everybody in the world loved New York, and loved New Yorkers, and I have to tell you, that was a very insulting statement that Ted made.
>
> – Fox Business debate, January 14th, 2016

Ted Cruz was outflanked here, and his body language - a subtle nod of his head - betrayed his surrender, the loss of his frame. He also clapped in applause for Donald Trump in this debate, and the hands are a more honest part of the body than the face.[23]

Now instead of someone questioning Trump's credentials on conservatism, people think of Cruz insulting New Yorkers and their resilience in the face of 9/11 – a now-sacrosanct trope in American history.

Trump didn't stop there however, because he mounted an offensive from a third front, attacking Cruz's questionable tactics in Iowa with his voter violation notices and his campaign staffers' spreading the rumor that Ben Carson had dropped out of the race. Trump could thus point to Ted Cruz as being a liar. The matter was made worse by the disciplining of the people in the Cruz campaign that were involved. This affirmed Trump's frame and shed more legitimacy in the public's mind to the suspicions he cast.

While Trump conducts his own attacks and offends everyone with his bombast, driving his opponents and the media into frenzy, his rock-solid frame prevents this outrage from being able to stick to him, because he does not affirm, deny, or buy in to the frames that his opponents try to set. He simply reframes every attack, every negative, into a positive for himself and a negative for his opponents. This is the phenomenon behind the phrases "Teflon Don" and "you can't stump the Trump." His mouth, far from being a loose cannon, is a finely-tuned precision instrument, and he is able to see many moves ahead in every battle of frames.

Donald Trump also closely follows Robert Greene's 18th law of power as narrated in his classic *The 48 Laws of Power*, which dictates that to achieve power, you must be constantly in the public gaze, as isolation allows others to set the frame against you (though he doesn't put it in those terms).[24] This has historically been one of Hillary Clinton's problems, as she has often refused to meet with the press and seems to do only the most carefully pre-selected interviews and staged appearances.

This may seem to the layperson to be helpful, but it is precisely the opposite, especially when she is already perceived as untrustworthy, because it allows others to hammer that frame home. They are allowed to dictate the frame on her.

Ultimately, by staying constantly in the public eye, as Louis XIV, who Robert Greene cites in outlining this maxim of power, did before him, Donald Trump has remained in control of the narrative, forcing the media to follow him.

In wrapping this chapter up, it's pertinent to return where it began, with

Steven Pressfield's *The Virtues of War.*

> Every battle is constituted of a number of sub-battles of differing
> degrees of consequence. I don't care if we lose every sub-battle, so
> long as we win the one that counts.[25]

Donald Trump recognizes this and sets his frame to handle it. By deliberately
courting outrage, by attacking his opponents with heated snark all the while
maintaining frame and doubling down, even when he's wrong or lying, he figures
he does not need to win the "logic" sub-battle. He doesn't need to win the beauty
pageant sub-battle of who has the best image or favorability rating either, because
he'll win the sub-battle that counts – that being in the realm where people really
make decisions, especially in crowds.

That last sub-battle consists of attracting the attention of prospects and then
completing the sale by getting your supporters to turn out for you and vote. So far,
Trump has done precisely that.

***

Takeaways:

1. Always be on the offensive in your efforts to impose and keep frame.
    The initiative is everything.

2. Concentrate your forces on the biggest threat, the most imposing
    obstacle, or the most daunting project. As Robert Greene says, focus
    on the mine that will yield the most.[26]

3. If things get dirty, you can take the course of framing your opponents
    as being antithetical to some primal, emotional mover. Concentrate
    on visceral, lower-brain factors such as their appearance, mannerisms,
    charisma, masculinity, femininity, or tribal/team loyalty.

4. Best of all, if you think you'll find yourself in a vicious battle of
    frames; make sure to scope out your competition prior to a prolonged
    engagement. Find a fairly innocuous word that has not been used
    before in such an offensive context,[27] something that fits your
    antagonist's character visually, sensually. Afterward, use that label to
    impugn him. "Low energy," "little Marco," and "lyin' Ted" are all
    labels that Trump has used successfully following these criteria.

5. Do not cower or apologize when you are attacked. Instead, counterattack. Counterattacking will maintain your frame more easily. You will be perceived well and it will make you bristle with confidence. Cowardliness or apologies in the face of attack are unconsciously seen by the public as admissions of guilt.

6. Know the desires and peeves of your key demographics and direct your counterattacks into frames that either affirm the former or display you as a champion against the latter.

7. The sour grapes approach[28] is in fact far superior to backtracking or apologizing. Grumble and dismiss the premises of attacks against you. Do not answer them. Do not attempt to deny them. Instead, grumble and counterattack with an entirely new premise and frame to impose on the conversation.

8. The mind follows the body just as much as the reverse. If you find yourself nervous while facing attack, I've found that simple shifts in the body, from waving a subtle, yet dismissive hand, to slowly shaking the head and narrowing the eyes, to simple walking or pacing, combined with thoughts of either the next action I'm going to take or active, talking thoughts of more emotionally positive images or experiences, reduce nervousness immensely. It's all-important not to freeze up. Being frozen in place creates more fear, as that is how we evolved to behave in the face of predators.[29] Instead, breaking up the freeze instinct forces your body and mind into fight mode. When attacked, or simply feeling nervous about an everyday situation in general, this is what you want to do. Notice that Trump is rarely still, even when attacked. He subtly shifts his eyes, head, or hands. Do the same.

4. Politics or Pro-Wrestling?

Some have compared Donald Trump's campaign to a WWE stunt. Indeed, Trump is a known fan of the professional wrestling promotion. He appeared center-stage at WrestleMania 23 and was inducted into its hall of fame in 2013.

Professional wrestling is generally condescended by most segments of the population for being "fake," but it's one of the best ways to study that elusive factor known as charisma and the art of working a crowd (which will be discussed in the next chapter). Politics has been compared, often derisively, to professional wrestling for a long while. Like it or not, attributes that can make someone successful in the WWE can be applied just as judiciously in politics. One famously successful political outsider, Jesse Ventura, was a professional wrestler.

If Donald Trump's iron frame is the bedrock of his tactics, his carefully cultivated charisma is one of the cornerstones of his operations.

Charisma is something that's esoteric to most. To them, it's something that you either have or you don't. It's something you just know when you see. This is actually only half accurate. Some people certainly have an advantage over others in the charisma department by their natural forces of personality, and Trump is obviously one of the men who naturally "have it," but charisma is also something that to a greater or lesser extent can be learned. Aside from being a natural, Trump is also conspicuous in applying the learned and proven techniques of charisma into his persona and campaign.

The first secret of Trump's charisma is his overall energy level, which is created by the sum of his body language, vocal cues, and avenues of speech. The energy of the crowd amplifies the effect and he plays it as he goes. Donald Trump is like a whirlwind. He sweeps you up with his bombast, but he can switch from bombast to a calm, almost somber demeanor, and then back again just as quickly. This unpredictability, the 17th of Robert Greene's *The 48 Laws of Power*,[30] adds to the overall charisma.

Joseph Roach, a professor of English and theater studies at Yale, opines that charisma is in some ways a state of being able to hold contradictory qualities simultaneously:

> Charisma is the power of apparently effortless embodiment of contradictory qualities simultaneously: strength and vulnerability, innocence and experience, and singularity and typicality among them.

> People need to resent their idols as well as to adore them, tearing them down even as they build them up. People seek out figures whose personalities broadcast contradiction because they make it easier for them instantly to gratify their own contradictory needs. One of those needs is for "public intimacy," the assurance that the person who's not like anyone we've ever met is just like one of us after all.[31]

Being angry, yet calm, talking about heated issues but being able to keep a smirk on your face, being a billionaire but also appearing like a regular guy – these are attributes of charisma.

This was seen in the lead-up to and immediately following the vote on Super Tuesday, March 1st, 2016. Through the last few days starting from the CNN debate on February 25th, the campaign took a particularly nasty turn, even by its own standards. Marco Rubio descended into insults about Trump's body parts, with Trump responding that he was "little Marco." It was not something alien to a schoolyard brawl.

Yet when the voting was counted and Trump won the night as he was expected to, instead of holding a massive rally to fire up his own supporters and perhaps knock his competitors, like Ted Cruz (whose rally almost centered more around Trump than him – domination of space in action) and Marco Rubio had done, he held a press conference in which his tone was far more measured and calm.

Donald Trump turned from high energy bombast to lower energy reassurance in a snap. The press conference was as close to perfect as it could have gotten. The only exception was Chris Christie's decidedly unenthusiastic body language and facial expressions.

This roller coaster ride – from schoolyard insults to presidential press conference, and all within the course of a few days, is charisma in a nutshell. The contradiction keeps people on edge. Donald Trump sets up his atmosphere well in advance. He is always anticipated and never ignored.

Another foundational pillar of Trump's charisma is his notorious vagueness. Though many candidates aren't exactly much better when it comes to discussing those 15 point policy plans that pundits love, and Trump has released a few such policy positions on his campaign website, his answers to questions are vaguer than those of his competitors.

One vague thing Donald Trump says is a cornerstone of his speeches – that America "is going to start winning again." It's going to win so much, in fact, that "we're gonna be tired of winning!" How will we do that? Well, the wall (a visual anchor – see chapter 6), and some tariffs, and by the way, "I'm gonna bomb the shit out of ISIS."

Donald Trump tells you what he's going to do, assumes a position of strength with his frame, adds some other charismatic factors seen here into the mix, and then allows you to just fill in the blanks with your own plan instead of his.[32] This is something Scott Adams remarked on in an interview for *Reason* in October 2015, but it goes even further. Trump's vagueness reinforces his charisma in your mind because you will obviously be biased in favor of your own frame of reference. By making up your own plan, Trump seems to display that he thinks just like you. Why not complete the sale and vote for him? He knows the desires of the voters he's attempting to build into an electoral coalition and then usually speaks in a general enough way to let them confirm their pre-existing suspicions.

Another great example of how Donald Trump uses vagueness to his advantage can be found in the education chapter of *Crippled America*:

> Getting an advanced degree or a medical education can put a young professional well over $100,000 to $200,000 in debt.

> If the students can't get enough scholarships or loan support, the parents have to step in, despite the risks to their own retirement funds. They may have to borrow the money, often by taking out a second mortgage if they have sufficient value in their home.

> We can't forgive these loans, but we should take steps to help them.

> The big problem is the federal government. There is no reason the federal government should profit from the student loans. This only makes an already difficult problem worse. The Federal Student Loan Program turned a $41.3 billion profit in 2013.

These student loans are one of the only things that the government shouldn't make money from and yet it does.

And do you think this has anything to do with why schools continue to raise their tuition every year? Those loans should be viewed as an investment in America's future.[33]

If you're voting Republican or you're a registered independent that leans that way, you're suspicious about government, especially the federal government, to begin with, and you usually want it smaller if you can choose. If you're a student or parent on the hook for these loans, or you're a student or the parent of one about to attend college, you realize how deep the financial burden will be. You know that the current program isn't working and that something needs to be done. Trump is talking to your problems. He's saying something needs to be done and, for those who desire small government, that the federal government is a problem. You begin to think of solutions immediately. Does Trump plan to end the federal student loan program and cease future loans? Does he want to work to get a lower interest rate for current loans? Does he want to lower the interest rates for future loans? Does he want to give a permanent deferment until students can find a good job? Pick one, none, or all. Any way, he thinks like you.

Donald Trump's campaign has also been fraught with repetitions. In a way, he's hit the sweet spot with his repetitions. All politicians repeat things, as it's the nature of their business, and repetition is known to influence decisions. Yet, too much repetition can be harmful to a campaign.

This was displayed by Marco Rubio in his infamous exchange with Chris Christie in a debate before the New Hampshire primary, when Rubio repeated the exact same phrase word-for-word four times in rapid succession, a gaffe widely blamed for his disappointing fifth place finish in the Granite State. It was almost as if Marco Rubio were programmed to regurgitate certain blocks of text typed into a playback machine.

Donald Trump repeats general themes – notably winning. "We're going to win on the border. We're going to win on trade. We're going to win against ISIS. We're going to win with the vets." Of course, he also repeats his infamous attacks so that they stick. By these repetitions, you are influenced, whether you know it or not. Where Marco Rubio sounds like a robot, Donald Trump sounds like a cheerleader. He cheers you on and makes you feel good as he tells you about what he's going to do. You immediately begin to fill in the blanks about how the country is going to start winning again.

Then there are the smaller things which Donald Trump does that influence, even if they don't go consciously noticed. The first thing to look at here is Donald Trump's masterful body language. Most human communication is nonverbal, with body language taking up the lion's share (as well as being the most truthful) while nonverbal vocal cues take up the majority of the rest.

Body language cues can be subtle or grand. For instance, Donald Trump has the widest range of hand movements of any candidate I've seen in the 2016 cycle. Most politicians bob a fist up and down and wave, at times adding another motion or two, like a gesture to an opponent in a debate. Donald Trump, on the other hand, varies a lot. He stretches his arms far and wide, taking up space and establishing dominance, asserting himself as the alpha male, the leader of the pack.

Pay attention to Donald Trump as he's sitting down for an interview; watch those powerful hands of his. You'll find that most often, he steeples his fingers together. This steepling is actually an indicator of high confidence.[34]

He points and makes motions toward supporters, often including a thumbs-up, either to an individual or to the crowd as a whole. These hand movements are signs of recognition which establish rapport. When Donald Trump infamously announced his "Muslim ban" in early December, 2015, he varied his hand motions as he did so. He first started with a semi-closed fist, went steadily to an open hand, went back to the semi-closed position again, back to an open hand that bobbed up and down, and then spread his arm wide.

These motions were subtle, but effective at anchoring his strong overall frame and calm voice when discussing a very serious threat - Islamic terrorism. His torso was also totally calm, advertising his overall ease when discussing a phenomenon which threatened every American, projecting himself as a strong leader capable of dealing with the issue.

Speaking of vocal tones, Donald Trump also has a very good command of those. He projects his voice very well, among the top tier of the 2016 candidates, and does so from his chest and diaphragm, not his throat. His general voice tone is very bombastic and energetic, underscoring his verbal communication and captivating the audience, but he also knows how to vary it. He can do so depending on what he's talking about at the time, as seen once again in his infamous "Muslim ban" proposal. He usually chooses to be upbeat, but when the time calls for it, can turn on a dime, going from bombast to somber and back again.

This vocal range, or range of tone, is an important part of overall vocal communications. If you can't vary this, you will be talking in monotone, and you might as well be Ben Stein.

Ted Cruz also has good vocal range, but he doesn't have quite the range that Trump has, and also can't vary his range at the snap of a finger like Trump can. You might have noticed that one of Ted's techniques is to go from a slow windup and then build to a crescendo to make his point. It's a good technique which creates anticipation, and it beats everyone else in the race…everyone except Trump, who does not build up, but just snaps, adding to his unpredictability factor.

Another important dimension in possessing vocal skills is pace. Think about how you usually talk for a moment. Do you go fast, slow, or medium? Donald Trump knows how to pace his voice to the situation. When he's repeating points about winning or talking about how he's winning certain demographics, he's usually tending toward a fast pace. When he's making a big point, like "we're going to build the wall, and it's going to be a great wall, believe me," he often goes more slowly to hammer the point home. He's also slower when he's talking about somber occasions, like the victims of illegal immigrant crime or Islamic terrorism, adding authenticity to the occasion and helping to create a bad feeling that most would like to be rid of, which Trump conveniently provides the solution for. He reinforces this with his calm body language and voice tones. In fact, one study done found that Trump's voice showed few signs of stress, unlike other candidates.[35]

Yet another dimension is volume. Is it loud or soft generally? How good are you at controlling it where necessary for effect? Donald Trump gets very loud when he's talking about his general promises and concluding his campaign speeches, but he gets much lower when discussing threats or tragedies.

Ted Cruz has good pacing, but not as good as Trump. He comes across as fake, calculated, and unnatural to many. His crescendo technique is a good example, despite its virtues. It is an example of strong volume and pitch control. It also leaves anticipation, but it's too obvious to some that it's preplanned, whereas Trump's turn-on-a-dime technique comes across as far more natural and spontaneous, even though it is also preplanned.

As for the rest of the field? It's generally a pretty terrible lot in terms of vocal communication skills.

Ben Carson: He puts you to sleep. His pace is way too slow and does not vary, his range is monotonic, and his volume is unchanging.

Marco Rubio: He sounds stressed and rehearsed – and this is so because his pace is way too fast and he doesn't slow it down. This is another reason why the moniker "little Marco" is so devastating – because his constantly fast pace makes him sound like a nervous little boy, a decidedly unmasculine manner of speaking. His projection is generally good, but his range is also dismal, and he usually does not vary his volume.

John Kasich: His volume is low, his pitch range is low (hence, monotonic), and his pace puts you to sleep.

Jeb Bush: His pace is very slow, his volume is low, and his range is terrible. He's not totally unchanging in any of these, meaning he's better than Kasich and Carson, but when combined with his bad projection (he does not project from his diaphragm) and awful body language, which clams up and displays nervous smiles constantly, it is a death knell.

Hillary Clinton: The woman with one of the most annoying voices in politics. Her range isn't bad, but not great, and when she tries to pitch into higher tones it makes her sound shrill. Her pacing is slow and usually does not vary. She can project very well, talking from her chest and diaphragm, but it leads up a blind alley because she can't really control her volume, which is almost always loud – but this only makes her look phony because the loudness looks like it's trying to compensate for something. The cackle she does when seriously questioned does not help matters.

Bernie Sanders: His projection is weak and this does not help him. His volume and range are generally stagnant, but he can pace well, varying as needed.

Out of this field, the only one that can compete with Trump is Cruz, and he is still inferior.

Trump also brings his audience along for the ride like no other candidate. Crowd psychology will be examined in greater depth in the next chapter, but he makes his audience part of the show, forging powerful spectacles that his supporters participate in.[36] In addition to forging social/tribal bonds, this creation of ritual spectacle makes Donald Trump the leader of the pack, the top person in the social hierarchy. It also allows his followers to identify with him, giving them all a stake in his success.

A recent example has been Trump getting his supporters to raise their right hands and swear that they would come out to vote for him. This creates a fun moment connecting Trump to his supporters as they both participate in the same ritual. More importantly, the "swearing ceremony" is a small action taken on the part of each member of the audience. In turn, that makes those members more likely to vote for Donald Trump, as taking small, repeat actions overcomes procrastination and doubt and gives people a sense of conviction to complete the task at hand.[37] Questions cease when action begins. This is related to a phenomenon that has often been associated with Benjamin Franklin, who remarked that getting someone to do a small favor for you will make it more likely that that person will do you a bigger favor in the future. In this case, the "swearing ceremony" is the small favor.

Yet, the most famous example of Trump leading the audience on and encouraging participation goes back to; you guessed it, the wall. At his rallies, he constantly asks the audience: "who is going to pay for the wall?!" It immediately and enthusiastically replies: "MEXICO!" Often, he asks it several times, establishing the pattern of repetition and emphasizing a visual, the wall in the mind's eye.

Another famous instance of this dynamic occurred prior to the Nevada caucuses, when the lights went off at one of Trump's rallies. Expertly maintaining his frame and not letting it bother him, Trump said that the lights were brutal anyway, and demanded that they be turned off. He quickly brought the audience into the act, goading them into chanting his demand to "turn off the lights!"

Trump has also on occasion thrown the famous, or infamous, hats with his campaign slogan on them into the crowd. This creates rapport, establishes Trump as the dominant figure, and rewards followers of the group, incentivizing them to continue to follow him and for more to come in.

Donald Trump also compliments his supporters as well as anyone that is "nice" to him, sometimes even alternating between complimenting and attacking the same entity, like a reporter or political opponent.

One time in December 2015, when a few Trump supporters began chanting the "can't stump the Trump" meme that took off on the internet throughout the year, he made numerous hand gestures at them, including a thumbs-up, thanked them, and said that he thought they were "rough protesters," basically calling them tough – the ultimate compliment in the Trump world.

He's also known to tell his supporters that he "loves them" at the end of his rallies, putting wind in their sails when many of them feel that they have no one fighting for their interests, a point Trump repeatedly hammers home by going after donors and lobbyists.

All of these things create an in-group sense of belonging, with Trump as leader of the group.

Rounding out the list of many charismatic techniques are subtle body language cues. Have you noticed the smirks, head tilts, raises of the eyebrows, and so on? Trump often does these in response to the crowd, basking in its adoration, which in turn makes it adore him even more, as his audience instinctively understands that these are markers of recognition. Trump is recognizing and rewarding his supporters with attention as well as preparing them for the next conversational thread.

Another famous example of this can be found in that laboratory of charisma, professional wrestling, when The Rock raises the "People's Eyebrow" in his promos. This is a response to the crowd, but it also creates anticipation for the next segment of the promo, bringing the audience where The Rock wants it to go. Trump does the same thing. His opponents don't.

Finally, Trump's eyes are typically narrowed, but with a dash of a smirk on his face. This creates, in effect a final contradiction – a frown with a smile. It's subtle, but it works, and it makes Donald Trump look like the leader of the pack – at ease and cool, yet determined. You will notice that Trump usually (not always, but usually) talks with squinted eyes and with that dash of a smirk on his face, rather than raising his eyebrows while making more serious expressions like most people do. He *does do* the latter (we all do), but more rarely than his competitors. This is a more charismatic way of speaking with someone. You're more at ease. You seem more confident. Thus, people are more drawn to follow your lead. Notice that among Trump's competitors, Ted Cruz does this the second-most often, while Marco Rubio's eyebrows (and thus eyes) are constantly raised. This makes him look like a nervous rabbit.

Yet, there's also one maxim of charisma that is perhaps more important than all of the things mentioned so far – connection. For all of the techniques and phenomena discussed so far, you may have noticed that each one connects in some way to the person on the other end of them, forging some kind of bond between Trump and his supporters, The Rock and his audience, or anyone else using the techniques on other people. Charisma begins by understanding and connecting with others, in general or specific ways.[38]

Even when outlining the connection between charisma and contradiction, Roach essentially outlined that the charismatic person can connect on a visceral level to the feelings of those he's influencing. When Donald Trump compliments his supporters, gives them gifts, fights their enemies, and captivates their attention with the previously outlined techniques, he's making an effort to connect with them, though not in a needy way. He knows what moves people and he takes action accordingly. He is confident enough to present himself just as he wants to be seen, without advertising any neediness. Even by using techniques of body and voice, Trump understands what connects to people, and he has made a conscious effort to forge that connection, whereas most politicians, or people for that matter, simply expect to be followed.

Ironically, this sort of honesty allows Donald Trump to be more manipulative. People will repay many times over the person that seems to actively take an interest in and fill the vacuum of their desires.[39]

These techniques and pillars of charisma dominate the feelings of the people, wrapping them around Donald Trump's finger, but it takes two to tango. In the next chapter, the dynamics of crowd psychology are explored, and with it, how Trump works from that side of the equation to make his charisma truly magnetic.

***

Takeaways:

1. Have a higher energy level than the people you're attempting to influence, varying for the occasion. If in a high energy environment, have very high energy, even higher than the other person or people. If in a lower energy environment, keep your energy at the appropriate level, but a bit higher than the other person or people. Take your audience by storm. It will enjoy the ride, as people are bored and looking for grand entertainment.

2. Charisma is connected with contradiction. Have seemingly contradictory characteristics and ambitions, whether slight or stark. You can be a crusader toward a cause but a bit of a rogue if kept in balance. With your verbal and nonverbal communication, be calm yet decisive, a rabble rouser, but a gentleman. These are but a few tropes you can hone in an effort to be a little contradictory. Just make sure you don't look like a clown. Finding your balance is key.

3. When making arguments to persuade people to act in the way you desire, keep them vague and general enough as to allow others to confirm a pre-existing suspicion (and you should always be researching the specific suspicions, fears, and desires in your prospects to make this technique even more powerful). This will create a connection where you both seem to think alike.

4. Repeating general, simple themes, like lofty goals and objectives with a smattering of ways to seemingly get there, will influence support. Just make sure you don't repeat things word for word, or you will end up looking like "Marco Roboto" (another negative meme that circled around Marco Rubio, especially after that New Hampshire debate debacle with Chris Christie). Stick with general, positive themes, like "winning" or "progress," as targets of repetition. In this, active verbiage is typically best.

5. Most communication is nonverbal. To captivate attention, what you say is not enough. Instead, use your entire body. Make a wide number of hand gestures, nods of the head, subtle smirks and glints of the eyes. Even better if you can anchor these body motions to the words coming out of your mouth. If you're talking about something sobering, remain calm, but display decisiveness. If you're talking about something upbeat, enhance that excitement with the appropriate gestures. Above all, do not appear nervous with your body language. Take up space – don't clam up.

6. Learn to vary your vocal cues. You should remember these four words: projection, range, pace, and volume – PRPV. You should work on varying all of these. If you can do so, you will be well above average in terms of having good vocal skills. If you can vary them all in accordance with the point being made in your verbal communication, you will be in the top tier of the population. Remember to project your voice from your chest and diaphragm, not your throat, and if you need to practice, do so by making podcasts or videos – they are excellent and can be done for free.

7. Bring your audience along for the ride. Get those you wish to influence to take a small, innocuous action on your behalf. Even a simple raising of the hand, turn of the head, or completion of a train of thought you were saying will forge a connection and make further action on your behalf more likely. This allows you to establish frame over those you seek to influence.

8. Create anticipation. Before making the crescendo of your biggest point, lower your voice to get your prospect to lean in. Then deliver it with either a booming roar or a soft, confident, suave grin. You can also use rhetorical questions, like Trump's infamous "who is going to pay for the wall?" to create anticipation. If copywriting, create a headline that conveys a sense of urgency – a benefit that is known, but can only be attained in a mysterious way that your prospect needs to know RIGHT NOW. One example might be "you'll never guess how easy it is to be more charismatic – these three open secrets will tell you how."

9. When speaking, try to keep the raising of your eyebrows to a minimum. By doing so, you are prone to looking nervous. Instead, train yourself to lower your eyebrows and make a smirk. You will look and feel (as the mind follows the body just as much as the reverse) more confident.

10. Compliment (but don't over-compliment) your followers or people who say nice things about you in contrast to the people you attack. The contrast will make others desire to follow you.

11. The most important aspect of charisma is connection. You must connect with your followers. Do not expect to be followed. Instead, talk to them, be among them, and reward them while expecting nothing in return. Little things go a long way. You must know their needs and pet peeves. This allows you to dominate space in their minds by talking about and acting on them.

5. The Crowd Shrink

The atmosphere of the current election cycle is decidedly anti-establishment. It's something this book covers in depth starting in chapter 7. Yet, atmosphere alone cannot account for the character of a mass movement. Someone needs to be able to work the crowd behind the movement, to channel it the way he wants it to go. Leadership matters.

In marketing, there's the old trope of first attracting attention and then retaining the interest of your prospect. Trump's charisma does both. But how does he grow his following – how does he begin to translate the operational level, which is where this narrative still is, into winning strategy?

The second cornerstone of Trump's operations is the crowd and the way he uses his audience to build itself. If Trump's charisma is the proactive part of the equation, the crowd is the reactive counterpart that expands his operations outward, establishes his public and media presence, and allows him to serve his strategic ends.

To put it simply, Donald Trump is a master of crowd psychology. He knows how to work a crowd and get it to work for him. The first thing that Trump realizes is the premise this book is based on – human decisions are mostly not made rationally. This is especially so in crowds. It all comes down to a simple fact of human nature – we all want to fit in.

One of the most poignant examples of Trump's understanding of crowd dynamics was at a rally in Iowa in November 2015. A big Trump issue has been wounded veterans and how unfairly they've been treated by the Department of Veteran's Affairs. While not an existential issue (see chapter 8), it's great for Trump, as no one had seized on it and it gives him a positive image – not the worst thing to have for a man with high unfavorable ratings.

At this rally, a wounded veteran told Trump that he was having a hard time receiving care from the VA, asking what he would do to improve the situation. Trump complimented him and his family and then went down from his podium to talk to them face to face. Afterward, he told the man to write down his phone number so that he would be able to "put pressure on the VA like you wouldn't believe," to thunderous applause.

Aside from the usual posturing of virtue and the more visceral distribution of a reward to a follower, Trump also increased the morale of all his other followers by this and many other actions.

Napoleon famously said that in warfare, the morale is to the physical as three to one. Occasions such as what Trump did for that wounded veteran increase the morale of all his followers, making them feel powerful and motivated. This will certainly incentivize them to come out to the polls to vote for him. They'll want more of those good feelings, which are reinforced by the crowd, the tribe. It's something far more powerful than calls to action based on policy, which most politicians engage in.

Most politicians either promise to solve a problem of policy - a logical brain engagement that gets you thinking instead of motivated and feeling good, or promise to transform your life economically, which gets you feeling good, but in the realm of the abstract. Donald Trump's actions, such as with that wounded veteran, telling his followers how much he loves them (often when no other prominent presence will), or by insulting a hated out-group like politicians or the media, create feelings of good cheer, team inclusion against another team, and establish the presence of a leader you want to march into battle behind. It is something very close to what Thutmose III did at Aruna.

As Robert Greene remarks many times in his The 48 Laws of Power, emotional states are contagious.[40] By changing the crowd's emotional state to what he desires, Donald Trump creates a call to action. He increases the audience's motivation to act on high morale, as seen in the case of the wounded veteran. These are feelings people like to continue, which they can do by electing Trump. He also creates anger and frustration — at the corrupt, incompetent establishment and the results of its actions which he calls disasters. Negative feelings are things we'd like to be rid of. How does Trump's audience rid itself of those feelings? By lashing out at what makes it angry — in this case politics as usual. How can this backlash be achieved? It can be achieved by electing Trump. The crowd amplifies all of these individual feelings which were already bubbling up inside each follower. On either end of the emotional spectrum, Trump wins.

Furthermore, in addition to raising morale generally, the above instances make his supporters feel that Donald Trump likes them. Though these two things obviously relate, the distinction is important enough to illustrate as separate concepts because they both matter in related, but still different ways.

When people believe that someone likes them, they are far more loyal, trusting, and ready to do that person favors.[41] This is a fact which Trump's poll numbers have tended to show. He has by far the most loyal base of voters of any candidate in the field with the possible exception of Bernie Sanders.

And more than anyone else in the race with, once more, the possible exception of Bernie Sanders, Trump conveys a genuine, everyday, unscripted likability to his followers. He takes kids for helicopter rides and seems to enjoy it, as seen at the Iowa State Fair, where most politicians only go because it's a necessity, and it shows. One such blatant display was when Jeb Bush was eating hot dogs there. Photo ops such as these are generally counterproductive. They attempt to convey a common touch, but since the Bushes of the world are decidedly uncommon, they backfire because they just aren't believable. Instead, staging a photo op displaying this un-commonality, but in a way that benefits the common people, is far better because it's vastly more believable. Donald Trump did this by giving those rides to the kids at the Iowa State Fair.

Trump tells his followers he loves them and seems to display it, fighting as hard for them as he can in their eyes. He also has his one on one moments which are brilliant, whether these moments are comprised of a fun sharing of jokes with individual members of his audience or of tender ones with that wounded veteran. Another such tender moment occurred recently in Wisconsin with the former Miss Wisconsin, Melissa Young, who had previously received a handwritten letter from Trump while struggling with an incurable disease. He also guaranteed her son a college education and, at the rally, insisted that the doctors would be wrong about her illness. He had another tender moment with her offstage.

Fake or not, Donald Trump is perceived by his supporters as genuinely showing that he cares about them and the country. This feeling is then reinforced and solidified by the emotional contagion of the crowd, which unconsciously enforces this tribal loyalty of rallying around its leader.

It's yet another advantage Trump has over the politicians he's outcompeting. By talking endlessly about the logical brain aspects of policy, most politicians don't convey the feeling that they actually like their supporters. Instead, those politicians are mostly talking about *themselves* and *their* ideas, rather than the benefits they want to deliver to their supporters because of how much they love them. The full implications of this will be shown below as well as later on in chapter 6. This avenue of engagement is certainly not going to have reinforcement from the contagion of the crowd. Thus, the crowd will not be its own institution actively on the side of Trump's competitors.

Using the crowd as an institution is the central concept of this chapter. It's part of a phenomenon called **social proof.**[42]

To put it simply, humans are generally followers. In another indictment of the worldview of human beings as individualist automatons shopping in a marketplace, humans take action not necessarily because they perceive it as beneficial for themselves, but because they see or are pressured by the actions of others. Have you ever felt pressured to do something you didn't really want to do because your friends were doing it, or found that you suddenly looked into a product that wasn't really on your mind but seemed cool because other people were using it? That's social proof in a nutshell.

Appeals to authority may be logically fallacious, but most human decisions are not made in the realm of logic. Authority, whether it emanates from the crowd or a prominent figure, motivates to action far more than the logical explanations of a product.

Donald Trump already established himself as an authority figure with his charisma and personal brand (seen in the next chapter). To perfect the trifecta, he uses the audience as a cat's-paw to amplify his authority, and build another, bigger audience.

In marketing, it's well-known that if you talk about the numbers of other people using your product, you will get a better conversion rate.[43] It induces the thought, "if other people are doing it, why not me?"

This correlates with a well-known experiment in crowd psychology. Let's say you set up an event, but there aren't any people waiting on the line for it. Because of this visual of the lack of a line, the first potential event attendant will be hesitant to get on the line. This is because he'll be wondering: "why isn't anyone else on the line?" This connects with the famous bystander effect, where no one helps someone in distress because no one else is doing the helping. It's almost like a game of chicken to see who takes action first.

However, once someone does take action and gets on the line, others find it far easier to follow. Afterward, still more come onto the line just because so many other people are there, and they are curious as to what it's all about.

The famous Stanley Milgram conducted a similar experiment wherein it was found that just one person looking up at a window would draw 4% of passersby to stop and look up. If 15 people looked up, 40% would stop, and a full 86% of people walking by would at least take a glance.[44]

Have you also noticed this same dynamic on online forums – how they can vary so much between low and high energy? It seems that when no one is on or posting, no one else posts either, but when a few people start to post in a thread, it suddenly takes off like a rocket! This is a great, everyday example of crowd behavior in action, particularly for the Millennial generation.

Demonstrating how many followers you have - the size of your audience - is the ultimate form of social proof. Trump plays the game better than any politician in the 2016 race, or for that matter, that I have ever seen.

The most famous example of Trump using social proof is his constant citing of his poll numbers, which he has been dominating since July 2015 against all expectations. He always talks about how many people support him. Once he began winning elections, he talked about how he won with every demographic – rich, poor, highly-educated, poorly educated, evangelicals, across racial lines, and so on. All of this achieves the same effect – social proof. So many people like Trump, so why not you too? Donald Trump himself has said that he would not be citing his poll numbers if he were losing. There's a simple reason for that – it would be an advertisement that no one likes a particular candidate, meaning people will be less likely to support that candidate because of that fact alone, even if they might like what a candidate says. This has often been termed the "electability" factor in politics. Despite the ivory tower saying that Trump was unelectable from the start, after he continued to dominate in the polls for months on end, the people at large began to disagree. The widespread support Trump was getting was evidence, as they perceived it, to the contrary, and his support subsequently rose higher. That is the power of social proof.

One particular instance that displayed Trump's mastery of social proof, and how he used it to pull the audience where he wanted it to go while using his charisma as the carrot, came at a rally in September 2015 in Virginia. Trump was talking about how he was leading the polls on every issue, including ISIS, an issue in which he had 49% in a still very crowded field. He pointed to himself (note the hand movements as discussed in the preceding chapter) and said, very clearly and relatively slowly (the slow pace helped him to sound authoritative on the issue), "we're not gonna play games."

This was all an anchor. He may as well have been saying "You want to kick ISIS ass? Join the Trump Train. 49% of the people agree with me in a crowded field." In addition, it created a very large in-group to work as a team against a much hated out-group, ISIS. That was not the only time an in-group/out-group dynamic was created at that very moment.

During this recitation, there were some protesters. Trump was calm and humorously dismissed the hecklers, knowing that his own supporters would cheer him on. He encouraged them while they did so, making motions and turning around to acknowledge everybody. He also used the opportunity to lambaste yet another out-group – the media, remarking that the presence of protesters were the only times the cameras turned to show the crowds at his rallies because "the press is so dishonest."

That's three out-groups denigrated in the same segment (ISIS, leftist protesters, and the media, all of which are hated by the Republican base), plus two examples of social proof – poll numbers and the size of the rally. His rallies are another avenue of such social proof in general, as Trump routinely cites their size and energy, reinforcing the "cool" in-group factor. He does this while talking about how few people show up at his opponents' rallies. This casts them as "uncool." It also incentivizes the in-group tribe to act and complete the sale by giving it an opposing tribe or group to defeat.

Yet another way Donald Trump displays social proof is with his secondary slogan, "the silent majority stands with Trump."

See what he just did?

If all those people stand with Trump, why not you?

Sloganeering (a form of headline copy) is a particularly insightful area in the study of crowd psychology. Does the slogan display social proof? Does the slogan play to emotions? Does the slogan motivate to action, to complete the sale, partly by thinking past it? One of my first lessons in marketing was in real estate, when I attended a seminar from Craig Proctor, one of the most successful real-estate brokers in the world. A key issue of import was that you, as the salesperson, must remove yourself from the equation. People may like a product that you're offering, but still avoid salespeople like the plague on instinct. Anyone reading this will have had such an experience.

In other words, as the salesman, you need to focus on the prospect, not the product, the *buyer*, not the *seller*. You need "to play the radio station WIFM – what's in it for me?"

Some other slogans in the 2016 campaign can be compared for effect:

Hillary Clinton: "Hillary for America."

Terrible slogan. It focuses on the seller, displays no social proof, does not motivate or have a call to action, and reminds you of someone most people dislike. To many people, Hillary is anathema to America, thus it gives those people a *negative* reaction.

Bernie Sanders (primary slogan): "Feel the Bern."

This one doesn't, in fact, get you to feel much of anything, which is in some ways even worse than a negative reaction.

Jeb Bush: "Jeb can fix it."

Reminds you of a man many dislike because of his negative social proof – his association with his brother. It does not have any feeling in it at all. It also focuses on the seller, not the buyer.

Lindsey Graham: "Ready to be Commander-in-Chief on Day One."

Utterly boring and too wordy. There's absolutely nothing in it for the buyer. Even Jeb's was better than this in that regard.

Ted Cruz: "Courageous conservatives reigniting the promise of America."

I don't believe that "courageous conservatives" is a particularly affective evocation of an in-group or at least a big enough in-group for general election purposes, so the social proof is limited. Furthermore, who is doing the "reigniting?" There's a call to action to the prospect, but it's muddled.

These were all bad. Here are a few better ones:

Marco Rubio: A new American century.

It's not bad. It's catchy, in part because it's short. It focuses on a vision, not the seller of the vision, and is vague enough to let the prospect fill in the blanks of that lofty vision with his own ideas. However, it does not have a call to action to prospects. Worse, it has a fatal flaw in the 2016 election cycle – it goes against the spirit of the times. It's too optimistic, when pessimism is spreading. In other words, Marco Rubio did not know his market well enough to make the proper offer.

Rand Paul: "Defeat the Washington machine. Unleash the American Dream."

This was a good slogan, as it denigrated a hated out-group (the Washington establishment), promised a good outcome, and invited the prospect to take action. It leaves a vagueness that others can fill in with their own ideas (the American Dream). In fact, it's among the best slogans I've seen in the 2016 cycle.

Bernie Sanders (secondary slogan): "A future to believe in."

Now we're talking! "A future" as well as "believe in" creates a call to action (as exemplified in the verb "believe") by promising the crowd something better than today, fitting the spirit of the times. It acknowledges the downtrodden emotions that many are feeling and are therefore looking for change. It's also appropriately vague, letting the prospect fill in the blank. It's similar to Barack Obama's "change we can believe in" slogan in 2008, which was a great one also (better than this, as "we" creates an in-group).

Yet, Trump's two slogans beat them all. "The silent majority stands with Trump" is a clear and unambiguous display of social proof and it creates an in-group to join. "Stand" is an invite to action, and as we know, taking the action of "standing" with Trump will make supporters more likely to do other actions on his behalf.

His primary slogan, "Make America Great Again," is about as close to perfect as any slogan or headline can get. It's catchy. It fits the downtrodden spirit of the times, but also promises something better and is a positive message. It's unambiguously about the buyer, not the seller, answering the WIFM question perfectly. It implicitly creates an in-group by allowing the prospect to identify himself with those who are making America great again. "Make" also creates a compelling call to action, a rallying cry for a vision that is also appropriately vague, allowing the buyer to fill in the blanks himself.

After creating these calls to action and touting his social proof, Donald Trump then goes on to repeat the general themes of the campaign in all his speeches, but these speeches also invite action, like "winning," or making America great again, or bombing ISIS, or building walls or infrastructure. These calls in turn create powerful social bonds, and the way he leads on his followers with thoughts of action and then rewards them are in essence rituals that forge the strong ties of the in-group, fostering loyalty and determination to defeat the out-group.

The best way to describe how Trump uses his mastery of crowd psychology as an institution supporting his operations can be illustrated best not in the news, but in fiction.

One of my favorite fictional series is *Ghost in the Shell*, in particular, the *Stand Alone Complex* iteration of the meta-series. The name of the show derives from the phenomenon of a standalone complex, which consists of completely unrelated copies working toward the same end with no communication between them. Given crowd behavior, more are due to follow the first efforts to achieve that end, even if for completely different reasons than the original actor/s, indeed, if there were any such originals at all. In the first season of the show, there was no original actor or action, but copies behaving in ways that they perceived the original actor would have been, which inspires them.

Perhaps the ultimate test of the ability of a crowd psychologist is whether he can engineer a standalone complex working toward a goal he wants. This is probably the ultimate antifragile social institution. How can it even be attacked when there are no principles or organized leaders to attack it from?

The Trump campaign fits many of the parameters of a standalone complex. Individuals that are totally unrelated, ranging from outright racists to progressives angry with Hillary Clinton, from traditional, paleoconservative nationalists to middle-of-the-road independents, to saboteurs from the left, to people who just want to see it all crash and burn, Donald Trump has essentially created a standalone complex, as vastly unrelated factions are all working in concert, for differing ends, to get him elected. He offers something to all of them, even if that offer is perceived as being destruction. Certain environmental factors were necessary to create these conditions, and they will be explored, but Trump pulled all the right levers to manufacture a standalone complex out of them.

One last thing can be said about crowd psychology and social proof. It was saved for last because the traditional way of understanding politics often views it as among the most important. Politicians do, on some instinctive level, understand social proof, and it comes in the form of endorsements.

These endorsements are usually viewed as crucial. As remarked upon, approval from authority figures is one form of social proof. To a neutral observer, your being associated with an individual that he considers to be high status automatically raises your own status in his eyes, even if he knows nothing about you. This is why men who are married or who have been seen with other women are more likely to be attractive to women, no matter what they look like. This is a phenomenon called "pre-selection" in seduction circles.

The magician Steven Cohen also proved this at his own shows, when he began handing out a biographical card showing the high-status people he had entertained previously. After he had done so, Steven Cohen described the audience's reaction to him as being "significantly better."[45]

In politics, endorsements are seen as being so important that Five Thirty Eight's Nate Silver, one of the most celebrated pollsters in the field, has mentioned that they are usually one of the biggest indicators of getting a party's nomination in presidential contests.[46] This was a major reason why he thought Trump's chances of securing the nomination were near zero. Yet, he may have it somewhat backwards, and Trump, who doesn't play by the normal rules, has hammered home the inherent weakness of this prognostication.

In South Carolina prior to the primary, Marco Rubio got two very high profile endorsements - the popular sitting governor, Nikki Haley, and the popular sitting senator, Tim Scott. They campaigned with him for days and raised his profile as much as they could, yet he lost to Trump by double digits come election time, and virtually tied with Ted Cruz.

In actuality, these kinds of high profile political endorsements probably *follow*, rather than dictate the polls. They can move them perhaps a little bit, but when other factors come into play, like the ones outlined in this book, they matter comparatively little in terms of securing popular support. The people doing the high profile endorsing often, if not most of the time, look where the polls are heading before making an endorsement, rather than coming out immediately in support of a certain candidate. This in a way is a political game of chicken, a bystander effect.

Compared to the massive social proof Trump displays – at his rallies, on his social media accounts, in his constantly-dominant poll numbers, and so on, these endorsements have not meant a thing. Indeed, Silver's hard-nosed statistical analysis is essentially a narrow ivory tower view of the universe in what amounts to visible light only, not the entirety of what can be observed along the full spectrum. He missed the importance of Trump's sales skills and his organic social proof, which he dismissed as a vague notion of "momentum." He missed where the political market was truly heading.[47]

A few days prior to Florida's primary on March 15th, Marco Rubio held a rally at a football stadium, expecting to draw a large crowd. In fact, the crowd he drew was pitifully small, fitting only inside the end zone. He went on to lose to Trump by nearly 20 points, despite being the sitting senator of the state and having many high-profile endorsements. Anyone viewing the picture of that rally would be suspicious about Rubio because of the smallness of the crowd alone, despite the high-profile endorsements. He would have been a lot better off hiring a huge number of actors.

When someone is seen as cool, as a winner, with a mass following behind him, others will follow simply because they want to be part of the new in-group, the winning tribe, too. Even high status backers behind someone or something else won't be able to dissuade such a massive following that is seen as having winning momentum. This fact ties in perfectly with the next concept, that of preference falsification and cascades.

Trump may be benefitting from another game of chicken of sorts, known as a "preference cascade." Since we all want to fit in, we hide views and opinions that we believe will result in our ostracism from society and our personal social circles. Yet, when the game of chicken ends, and some critical number of people begin to express these seemingly heretical views, the concurrent game of "preference falsification" – where the fearful hide their true beliefs behind a mask that is seen as more socially acceptable – also ends. The true beliefs of a seemingly small number appear to be not so small in number at all, and those who were wavering before now have the courage to show their true selves. This cascade then demands action, forcing the ethos of the day to change.[48] When viewing Trump's rallies, the "silent majority" slogan is so incredibly effective because this is indeed often what appears to be occurring, one rally, one press conference, or one primary victory at a time.

Trump took this social proof, built huge audiences, created a sense of belonging, anchored his followers with gifts, fostered high morale, induced negative states which he could then solve, used his personal charisma, and captivated the public with calls to action toward an optimistic end that bypassed the salesman and answered radio WIFM – what's in it for me? In the end, he took his plethora of followers and engineered a standalone complex against the establishment that could not be attacked, forcing a reckoning with the hidden desires of the electorate due to the preference cascade it caused.

In essence, Trump knows that people operate in stories. Trump made each follower of his the protagonist of his own story – as part of a great team to achieve a great end by making America great again. It's not only about Trump making America great again; it's also about *his followers* making America great again. Trump constantly talks in terms of "we." "*We're* going to make great trade deals. *We're* going to stop illegal immigration. *We're* going to make America great again folks! *You're* going to be part of the movement to take back *our* country!"

The crowd is an underappreciated institution, even in a supposed democracy. Instead, the talk has been all about donors this and authority figures that. When Trump was able to use the crowd in a way not seen in many years, his opponents were vastly outmatched.

At Trump's rallies, he talks about endorsements like Carl Icahn and recently Chris Christie and Ben Carson, but he usually shows his social proof as being the public, the crowd, at large. Even more recently, he's stated that he doesn't need Ted Cruz's endorsement because he "has the support of the people." There's nothing more democratic (small d) than that. The only candidate of 2016 who has been able to do this to a somewhat similar extent is Bernie Sanders.

Yet, Trump's social proof didn't arise from nothing. He came into the race with a huge brand behind him and he has done more to cultivate that brand and shape it into something politically distinctive than anyone else. That is the subject of the next chapter.

***

Takeaways:

1. Increase the morale of your team by offering giveaways and promising to solve very personal problems or by touting your ability to achieve their desires. Display that you are a fighter on their side and show tender, loyal support. Offer for your audience to keep those feelings of good cheer by doing what you want it to do.

2. Above all, show your supporters that you like them. Personally relate to your audience's desires and experiences. If you must, you can often embellish stories of your own and relate them back only very remotely – the most important part is that you give off an enthusiastic, sincere vibe. "That reminds me of…" would be a good place to start if you need a quick tip. Mirror the exact language of your supporters. Talk to each individual as if he's the only other person in the world.[49]

3. Get your audience angry at a visceral issue or out-group and offer a solution to alleviate that anger, that being for your audience to do what you want it to do.

4. If selling a product or service, mention, if possible, an impressive number of other people using it. Convey this with as much evidence as you need to. Use the size of your audience to build itself.

5. Create a distinct team or tribe, partly by defining what that team's opposition team is. Consciously cultivate this team image and inclusion by identifying yourself as part of the team or in-group. Use "we" and "our" in relation to accomplishing goals and defying out-group opponents. Create symbols of team distinction, such as Trump's hats.

6. When creating headlines or slogans, make your message not completely vague, but vague enough that it will allow others to fill in the blanks with their own cherished ideas, as also discussed in the previous chapter. Display social proof in your headlines. Identify the opposition or a lofty, optimistic, high-morale vision to obtain. Call your audience to action by using easily identifiable verbs, like "make," "do," "change," or "believe." Make sure your headline fits the spirit of the times in your marketplace. Above all, have a good headline or go home.

7. Lead your followers with thoughts of action or actual action in itself, especially in relation to an out-group. This will create an extremely powerful social bond between them as well as with you. You will be established as the commander, the king.

8. Give a wide swathe of demographics reasons for supporting you in your strategic aims. Attempt to engineer a standalone complex. Keeping some vagueness and ambiguity will make it harder for others to perceive you as pandering and easier for strange bedfellows to support you. Above all, make your benefits irresistible to a wide range of people.

9. Appeal to authority. Display testimonials or, better in the digital age, pictures with high-status figures using your product or service, or other markers of endorsement.

10. Advertise yourself, your product, or your cause as being associated with victory, or something that will make victory possible for your prospect. Combine this with your social proof and other calls to action.

11. Be a true friend, one that is willing to listen to people's real desires, no matter how incorrect it may seem to the prevailing orthodoxy of the time. This will create an instantaneous connection – and thus charisma for you. In these surveys of yours, another arsenal for your information machine, you may well be able to position yourself to benefit from a coming preference cascade. This is highly related to the pendulum phenomenon discussed in chapter 9.

12. We all operate in our own personal stories, the narrative of our own lives' journeys, the hero of a thousand faces. Make your prospects feel like they are the protagonists on their own great journey which conveniently intersects with yours. Convey yourself as an integral character in their epic story, which includes them doing what you want to have done.[50]

6. Making it Personal

Well before he got into the race, Donald Trump had support and wild speculation behind him. A few months before he announced, he was already polling at around 5% - impressive for a crowded field in which he still had not even thrown his hat in. When he stated early in 2015 that he would be "making an announcement that was going to surprise a lot of people" in a few months,[51] he had the luxury of creating anticipation and relying on that to generate attention, where most candidates for president who would have done the same thing, aside from Hillary Clinton and perhaps Jeb Bush, would be ignored.

That's because Donald Trump already had a proven personal brand.

The term itself has been somewhat popularized at the grassroots by Mike Cernovich. He describes it this way:

> Begin thinking of ways to distinguish yourself from the rest of the people in your office or workplace. They are generics. You are your own brand.

> While my message may not be suitable for the masses of men and women who live lives of hopelessness and despair, I do have a message. My message is one of unapologetic self-development. I don't apologize for seeking to better my life and I do not expect you to make any apologies for your life.

> You don't need to be an author or public speaker to think of yourself as having your own brand.[52]

We've been hearing a lot of talk about how the internet and social media in particular makes our personal and professional lives interconnected as never before. The infamous "social justice warrior" mobs using social media as a weapon against opponents and scoring scalps is good evidence of this. The New York legislature took up a bill a few years ago that would make it illegal for employers to search the social media feeds of employees and prospective employees without their consent.

Yet this can also work greatly in your favor. Appeals to authority work on an audience, and it is now within everyone's power to publicize themselves as an authority figure, whether that be on a niche topic or in broad categories. The general public now has the power to bypass the gatekeepers, form their own media outlets, build themselves out as a brand, and market products. It's changed the publishing and music industries. This book itself was published through the power of my own outlets, and none of its kind exists from a traditional publisher. Successful Instagram models now often make more than those signed with traditional agencies. YouTube delivers the power to create your own television station and news network.

By working through your own websites, blogs, and social media outlets, and by learning some marketing starting with the lessons discussed in this book, it is now within everyone's power to have an empire behind their names, to become a trusted authority. By doing so, more people will be willing to buy from you, and you will become an entrepreneur. This is the power of a personal brand.

Donald Trump bypassed the traditional political gatekeepers by the power of his own personal brand. Though he made his name well before the developments discussed above, he is his own empire. He does not require the approval of anyone else to do what he does, which also allows him to dictate the power of perception. He does not need to go to CPAC to make a name for himself or stand on the Senate floor or before the media. Donald Trump is his own man, his own authority.

Trump understands this concept very well. As mentioned previously, he puts the monetary value of his own name at $3 billion. Like many statements from him, this should be taken with a grain of salt (or more accurately, as you should know by now, as a ploy to dominate space), but it illustrates that he understands the value of his name and how he can use the empire around it to his own advantage.

His name and the authority surrounding it gave Donald Trump a tremendous edge at the start of the race, as illustrated earlier. Everyone knew who he was and had known for over 30 years. The celebrity phenomenon may be lambasted, but it is real, and it allows you to get away with things other people would not ordinarily get away with. It is no different in politics.

Aside from the obvious examples of Arnold Schwarzenegger and Jesse Ventura's successful gubernatorial campaigns, the candidate who is better-known usually wins the election, not least of which because he usually has more money, as more people are willing to finance him. The candidate with the better name recognition benefits from the fact that people trust things that are familiar to them. People will vote for and donors will donate to the familiar. These are a few reasons why incumbency is such an enormous advantage in securing reelection, even when institutions such as Congress are currently despised by almost the entire population. Despite consistently low approval ratings (usually hovering around 10%) for over a decade in both the Bush and Obama administrations, those same people usually keep coming back to Washington, don't they?

Market power, the familiarity of brands, works, even if the other brand might be better. Think about all those times you were shopping for something you needed and you saw two products side by side. Did you usually base your decision off of price or off of habit or familiarity with a certain product compared to another? I'll bet it was the latter.

This is yet another blow to the rational actor hypothesis.

Donald Trump had this huge advantage in market power and familiarity from the get-go. Everyone was familiar with him. Everyone saw him as an authority figure. This is also why, despite repeated attacks against him and his own gaffes, his standing in the polls has not gone down much, because people already had set impressions of him.

Trump also had another advantage. He was largely a political unknown before entering the race. He made comments on politics and policy, often contradictory over the years, before, but that was not the Trump brand. The Trump brand was in business and deal making. He was then able to frame that image of a successful businessman and deal maker as someone who would be able to bring common business sense to Washington and end gridlock by negotiation. He then defined and focused this image and authority onto key issues of his choosing. He also did not waste any time in dominating these issues with his bombastic reputation.

While Trump's lesser-known opponents, including Jeb Bush, were explaining who they were and what their message was, he did not need to waste such valuable time. He already had authority in the buyer's eyes. Now he just needed to go directly to the sale, whereas everyone else had to explain who they were and establish authority to overcome logical objections first. This worked doubly to Trump's advantage when it's likely that lesser-recognized brands do not benefit as much from repetition in advertising as more familiar brands do. In fact, they may even be hurt by such repetition over time.[53] This could explain to a large degree why Trump was not what most media figures and academics, including me, thought he was at first. Almost everyone thought he was the "summer flameout" insurgent candidate, the type that quickly rises to the top of the polls but then craters a relatively short time later. These insurgents – the Michelle Bachmanns and Herman Cains of the world, were unfamiliar brands, and the "bump" they received from their advertising brought them up initially. Yet, because they were unfamiliar brands, their ad repetition proved less effective and then counterproductive over the long term, as viewers experienced "wearout," began to formulate counterarguments against them, and perceived their ad tactics negatively. These thoughts then aversely impacted the public's perception of the candidates' personal brands themselves.[54] Consequently, they cratered. Trump, in contrast, fit the demeanor of more established, familiar candidates in politics, as everyone knew who he was from the beginning, and his poll numbers reflected as much. While Trump was the frontrunner, he had a solid base of support that expanded and at times contracted more slowly over the months leading into the primaries. This support was consolidated further when opponents dropped out after voting began. This is in fact typical of a traditional candidate, even though Trump is an insurgent by the standards of party politics. Additionally, Trump was less susceptible to negative perceptions from the get-go, despite his controversial tactics, because of his immensely familiar and authoritative personal brand.

Brand familiarity and authority, it seems, truly does make all the difference in the world.

When it came to selling in the campaign, Donald Trump anchored his personal brand to human, rather than abstract qualities. He talks about visuals and relatable stories rather than "policy specifics," which only pundits and talking heads really care about. While others tout policy proposals and much ballyhooed "specifics," Trump understands to focus on the buyer instead. In other words, Donald Trump focuses on *benefits* (how the voters' lives will ultimately be changed by voting for him), not *features* (the logical features of policy prescriptions people will get by voting for a candidate).

The best example of this is with the lynchpin of Trump's campaign, the wall. It's not only gonna be a wall, it's gonna be a GREAT WALL. It's gonna be a big, beautiful wall, with a big fat door for people to come in, but legally.

Rulers throughout history dating back to the time of the pyramids have used great building projects to solidify power. Grand monuments keep the ruler firmly in your mind and you associate this visual greatness with that ruler's initiative and strength. When you think of Franklin Roosevelt, one of the things you think of is Hoover Dam. When you think of Dwight Eisenhower, one of the things you think of is the interstate highway system. The more things change, the more they stay the same.

Trump anchored his personal brand in a political context immediately to this great visual that would solve a problem people were complaining about for decades. What a glorious solution! It's even better in that it anchors back to the Trump brand that everyone knew already – Donald Trump is a great builder. He was already an authority on building, so why wouldn't he be able to build a wall?

In contrast, Donald Trump's opponents, who were still trying to prove they were authorities on *anything*, tried to sell their policies and overcome objections which arose partially due to the lack of their being perceived as authority figures. They tried to sell the features of their policies. They were talking about how their tax plan would do X, Y, and Z. This is abstract and logical, and these features do not necessarily convey benefits – how to solve a problem or achieve a desire in an immediately perceivable way. Instead, Trump was selling the benefits of his policies from the place of his own authority. He was in every conceivable way light years ahead of his competitors from the very beginning and he immediately solidified that lead by picking the right issues to sell the benefits of his candidacy on (see chapter 8). When others were talking about entitlement reforms that would do this, this, and this, Trump was talking about building a wall that would instantly stop illegal immigration. The Trump brand in politics is associated in the minds of his supporters with *solutions*, not *policy*. The solutions are as grandiose as the man himself. His reputation did the talking for him. Trump and the wall are one.

In terms of personal brands, Trump's opponents do not compare well:

Hillary Clinton: The only person in the race who had a comparable personal brand to Trump in terms of reach and name recognition. Like him, everyone knew who she was from the get-go and had known for 25 years. Unlike Trump however, Clinton's only authority in the public mind is on dishonesty. What do you think about her when you hear her name? For most, the answer is corruption, age, a has-been, chaos in the Middle East, shady shenanigans at the Clinton Foundation, Benghazi, and now, the email scandal. The *best* thing that's thought about her is that she's Bill Clinton's wife, but this is not particularly helpful in building the kind of needed coalition to win a general election. Whether these negatives are legitimate or not is irrelevant, as remember, that is a distinctly "logical" argument, not the real force that moves people to make decisions. Even with her high name recognition, she lost in 2008 to Barack Obama (who possesses many of Trump's qualities), and is having a tough primary fight against Bernie Sanders this year. If the Democratic field were stronger, she would lose again.

Jeb Bush: He might not be such a bad character himself, but his brother totally ruined the Bush brand. When most people think of the name "Bush," they think of the war in Iraq and the economic collapse of 2008. Jeb Bush might have done a decent job as a governor, but that is again a distinctly logical consideration. Most Americans want nothing to do with the name "Bush" (or Clinton for that matter). Jeb Bush had a lot of money, but as soon as it appeared that there was a viable alternative in Donald Trump, people took the opportunity to shift allegiance. Frankly, Bush's weak performance over the course of his campaign leads one to believe that the Republican base might have jumped ship for someone else with or without Trump, though it would not have been as big of a rout.

Marco Rubio: He had name recognition in some conservative and Tea Party circles, as he was part of the GOP victory of 2010, but he wasn't as widely known nationwide as some of his other competitors. This forced him to play catch-up from the start. His name is also associated with the ominously-worded "Gang of 8" immigration reform bill of 2013. This was where he cooperated with figures anathema to the Republican base like Senator Chuck Schumer of New York, and in the context of something dubbed with the word "gang." To make matters worse, this occurred alongside a subject matter that many believed would be "amnesty" for illegal immigrants, another bane to the Republican base. This is an almost perfect storm of horrible branding. It's frankly surprising that Marco Rubio got as far as he did, though with the "establishment" field so weak, his youth weighed somewhat in his favor.

Ted Cruz: He was probably more well-known to the general public than Rubio and some others, but not in a good way. Ted Cruz is heavily associated with the government shutdown of 2013 in an era where most people are angry at the dysfunction and gridlock in Washington. Additionally, he is strongly associated with the religious right, an electorate of declining influence increasingly viewed negatively by the general American population. This is not a base from which to form a winning coalition.

Chris Christie: He would have been a strong contender a few years ago. He should have run in 2012. He had a high national profile as an authoritative, tell-it-like-it-is, tough Republican governor in a blue state that had formed a strong coalition in his 2013 campaign for reelection that included a sizable slice of the minority vote, something of high priority to the Republican Party after its 2012 "autopsy." Unfortunately for him, his brand was soon afterward tarred with the

"Bridgegate" scandal and has not recovered since, even if it appears that he had no direct involvement in it. Once more, logic takes a backseat.

John Kasich: Has a virtually unknown brand, despite his long and distinguished career. He also entered at the worst possible time, after Donald Trump was already dominating the conversational space. This gave him effectively no opportunity to establish himself as an authority on anything because no one was paying attention to him.

Ben Carson: He had a show on Fox News, but that station has actually had declining viewership (much like the rest of the traditional media). He did seem to successfully establish himself as an authority – on ethics and morals above the fray, a good contrast to Trump, but he could not establish himself as authoritative on strength, which mattered a lot more after the Paris attacks on November 13th, 2015.

The only one who comes close to Trump in terms of running on his personal brand is **Bernie Sanders,** who was a virtual unknown but who has built a brand around himself based on his sense of integrity and fairness, which was a good contrast to the perceptions centering on Hillary Clinton's brand. Like Trump, he catapulted his brand on some of the existential issues the country is facing. He built up his authority to the point that when you hear his name now, you immediately think of the economic malaise facing so many Americans and his ways of fixing it. In effect, Bernie Sanders established himself as an authority on economic inequality and forced Hillary Clinton to address it because of his spatial dominance on it. The fact that he's done as well as he has, even when the deck is squarely stacked against him while additionally lacking some of Trump's attributes, says much about the current state of left wing politics, as will be discussed in the next few chapters.

Sanders' major mistake during this campaign has been to not more forcefully attack Hillary Clinton's reputation and brand and her numerous vulnerabilities. Donald Trump has defined and attacked his opponents' brands relentlessly, most notably Jeb Bush's, until they were all essentially crushed. Low-brow, but as seen in the second and third chapters, it works. If Sanders had decided to do this, particularly regarding Clinton's less-than-perfect record on issues relating to African-Americans, he probably would have done better. He could have easily associated her more forcefully with the disproportionate affect that trade agreements like NAFTA and the proposed TPP, which she has championed in the past, have on the black community. Trump already staged a potential general election attack on Clinton's shady record with women relating to her husband. It caused her to immediately back off from her attacks on him, where she called him a "sexist."

Rest assured, in a general election, Trump will not make the same mistake Sanders made.

***

Takeaways:

1. Realize that in the present day and age, you can create your own business and brand through the establishment of your own media outlets.

2. People inherently trust authority. Logical objections are muddled in the face of it. Therefore, build your personal brand on your outlets by establishing yourself as an authority on something related to the demographics you wish to influence. Ask yourself what you know and how you can make it interesting. Build from there. Always keep in mind that you have a unique perspective and experiences which can never be duplicated. Others will find that information valuable if you present it properly.

3. In addition to trusting authority, we usually trust the familiar. Hence, you should become a trusted voice and a valued member of the communities around your topic/s. If you are an unfamiliar brand, focus on subtle advertising. Becoming a trusted voice is crucial. Take a content marketing strategy, where you build trust and provide value while featuring products sparingly.

4. Perception is reality (hence why guilt or status by association works). Ingrain in yourself that when influencing people, you are operating in the realm of perception. This gives you an almost godlike reality warping power – as perception is something that you can mold and craft to your desires. Be liked and you will already have an advantage in molding perception. You can also use your haters as tools by castigating them as an out-group to your preferred in-group. You will thus be perceived as a fighter. The haters are obviously mad at you about something, right?

5. Anchor your brand around problems that people want to solve or
    secret desires that people have. Your goal is to get people to easily
    perceive how what you're offering (see chapter 8) will solve a problem
    or fulfill a desire they have. Emphasize sensual solutions and benefits
    over the logical features of what you're selling. Instead, logical
    features are merely meant to explain an easily perceivable benefit and
    why your product will be of use toward achieving those benefits.[55]
    The more concrete and sensual the benefits appear, such as in the
    form of photos or videos, the better.

6. When confronted by an enemy, attack his reputation and his brand,
    not a defective feature of a policy or product. Show how he will not
    be able to deliver the benefits he is promising his audience. Be
    prepared for a counterattack. Your own reputation among the
    demographics you seek to influence must be spotless, or you must
    have a sufficient level of support that the attacks won't matter (see
    Robert Greene's 5th law in his *The 48 Laws of Power*).[56] This is why
    building authority and likability is so important – they translate
    directly to the trust factor. Do not forget the power of frame and
    language, or of tarring your attackers as part of a nefarious out-group
    conspiracy. Always remember that your goal is to win the sub-battle
    that counts, in this case, with your key demographics.

7. The Popular revolt of 2016

Background:

For all of Donald Trump's sales skills, for all his charisma, his social proof, his personal brand, his media domination, his masculinity, and so on, he would not have been able to have the success he currently enjoys were it not for the contemporary social climate.

There's an age-old controversy in the study of historical events. Is history defined by the man or the moment? Are there, from time to time, "great men" that change history in their wake, or are these so-called "great men" inevitable, creations of the social atmosphere of the time in which they live? The answer can only be a mixture. History is a synthesis of man and moment. Social atmospheres fulminate outward from complex conditions, but each great turning point is given its unique stamp and place in history by the leaders that guide the crowd to action to meet the challenges of the time.

Donald Trump has employed a wide range of skills and talents which he utilizes to dominate space on the tactical and operational levels, but those are all a means to an end. The latter chapters of *Stumped* zoom out to examine the strategic level. How will Donald Trump get elected? To what end is he expending his tactical and operational resources? There is a wide array of reasons that Donald Trump can claim to be the right man, but to answer these questions; it's imperative to examine the moment.

The 2016 election cycle is unlike anything seen decades. All indications are pointing to this being a black swan year. Both the Donald Trump and Bernie Sanders campaigns are clear indications that the currently established way of doing politics, what Bernie Sanders calls "establishment politics and establishment economics," is collapsing. Some call this the sixth party system, which may now be collapsing in the revolt of 2016. This election cycle may bear witness to the beginning of a transition to a seventh party system. This will be covered in greater detail in the 11th chapter.

The Popular Revolt of 2016 is so named because we are possibly seeing, for the first time, the establishment in both parties being overrun by waves of populism. Insurgent candidates have been a common feature in American politics. Usually they are defeated due to a lack of various factors seen in the preceding chapters, most often name recognition and by extension, media coverage and advertising effectiveness. Sometimes these insurgents leave lasting influences, but in 2016, they are seriously threatening the established order in both the Republican and Democratic Parties.

"Populism" is a term that is much-denigrated and has been through history. This is because the term itself derives from "populare" in Ancient Rome, where the traditional aristocracy of the senatorial class, the "optimates," squared off against such early populism, which it considered vulgar. The parallels are indeed very eerie. They are almost a carbon copy.

The Roman Republic was usually administered by the optimates, who acted through the aristocratic institutions like the Roman Senate. They were often opposed by the populares, who wished to act through "the popular" institutions closer to the general public. While the populares at times wished to push through reforms in favor of the people at large and the optimates defended the wealth of their class, it would be a mistake to view this through contemporary lenses, as the populare or optimate stances were often simply ploys for power by an always-competitive Roman aristocracy.

Despite that important difference, a more important similarity remains. Populist politics, as seen in the populare faction, first grew in Rome in response to a period of globalization associated with Rome's foreign conquests after the successful conclusion of the Second Punic War in 202 B.C., which in turn concentrated wealth and power upward. In this regard, the Popular Revolt of 2016 is just another iteration of an age-old struggle in history. There's nothing new under the sun, as the old saying goes.

The popular revolt seen on both sides of the political aisle in the current election cycle is a response to the latest period of globalization that has been underway since the 1970's. Dissatisfaction with both political parties has been high since the second Bush administration. A plurality of Americans now belong to neither political party. A common complaint is that no matter which party gets elected, nothing ever really seems to change. This was made manifest to a great deal of people, particularly the young, after the election of Barack Obama. He disappointed a wide swathe of the American public.

Why does nothing ever seem to change? Why do Democrats and Republicans oppose each other on comparatively minor issues like abortion or tax rates, but everything fundamental seems to remain the same?

The reason is because both parties have in fact merged into essentially a single party – the party of globalization at any cost. This means that the optimates, the established elites in both the Democratic and Republican Parties – the Bushes, the Clintons, the Romneys, the Obamas, and so on, are in lock-step on the issues related to globalization. The full manifestation and consequences of this will be discussed in the next chapter, but it is because of this similarity amongst the optimates at the most elite level that nothing ever seems to really change.

This is not a uniquely American phenomenon, as the rise of nationalist and far left parties in Europe, like France's Front National, The United Kingdom's UKIP, Greece's SYRIZA and Golden Dawn, the Netherlands' Party for Freedom, Spain's Podemos, Austria's Freedom Party of Austria, Sweden's Sweden Democrats, Denmark's Danish People's Party, Germany's Alternative for Germany, Poland's Law and Justice Party, and others have shown. All of these parties have one thing in common – they are "Euroskeptic" parties. They oppose the continued accretion of powers by the European Union and wish to return more power back to national governments. They reject various facets of globalizing influences which seem to only benefit the wealthy and well-connected.

In the post-World War II world, an era of consistent moderation in politics, particularly after the collapse of Communism, the dominant political forces have been center-left and center-right parties, shifting from one to another periodically. However, in recent decades, these parties throughout the world have seemed to merge into a single party in the ways that count. They also seem incapable of answering the challenges or meeting the desires of their electorates. In fact, many of the elites, the optimates in these traditional centrist parties, have begun to actively defy and even condescend to their own people and voters when challenged. Mitt Romney's anti-Trump speech after Super Tuesday, and Cologne Mayor Henriette Reker's comments that German women should "keep strangers at an arm's length" and that "people didn't understand the process of globalization underway" in response to the Cologne sexual assaults on New Year's Eve are good examples of this.

These elites, the optimates for globalization at any cost, are seen by broad swathes of people throughout the world as being arrogant, out of touch (and therefore uncharismatic), duplicitous, and greedy. This is the powder keg that has been building up for decades, and it has exploded into populist revolts across the world. In Europe, they take place in the form of the Euroskeptic parties mentioned above. In the United States, where the electoral system is not disposed toward the formation of separate parties, they take place in the form of insurrections within either party, as seen in the candidacies of Donald Trump and Bernie Sanders.

As left and right in the form of the centrist, supposedly moderate parties have merged in the most fundamental of ways into the stalwart, implacable cheerleaders for globalization, new opposition forces have emerged. The struggle of our time is not between left and right, but between nationalism and globalism – localism versus globalization. Where does power lie? How should people govern themselves? How should they shop? What are their very identities?

The optimates, the established governing forces with power in the mainstream, centrist parties, are almost all globalists. The revolt of the populares currently underway is composed of nationalists, or localists, even if they may not refer to themselves by such labels. The common thread between all currently revolting variants of populism is that they are opposed in whole or in part to the race for globalization, even if they may have different reasons for their stances and different solutions to the problems arising from it.

The Racket:

Barack Obama ran an excellent campaign in 2008 and an effective, but less convincing reelection campaign in 2012. You may have noticed that Barack Obama, especially the one seen in 2008, possesses many of the sales skills that Donald Trump does. It is partially what allowed him to defeat the Clinton machine. Yet, Barack Obama turned out to be a false hope, a false leader for the populares. Aside from him being a proponent of globalist policies, a big reason for why he proved to be a false hope to so many is because he was not independent of the power structure centered on the donor class. Barack Obama needed to raise money to get his name out there, build his brand, take himself to the public, and win elections.

Yet this donation structure is the means by which the optimates entrench themselves and propagate their power. As so many political scientists rightly remark, the candidate that spends the most money almost always wins the election. This is made more important in a post-*Citizens United* world, where essentially all restraints on money in politics are removed. This allows for total political warfare. It is in this doling out process that favors are distributed and alliances are made, which is then the key factor influencing decision-making in government for the next term.

To mark a man out as a distinctive leader of a popular revolt, he must therefore be separate from this power structure. Enter Donald Trump. With a net worth of anywhere from $4.5 to $10+ billion (depending on who you want to believe), the fundraising power structure is irrelevant. Donald Trump can fund his own campaign. He therefore does not need to answer any external favors from donor networks. Donald Trump does do some crowdfunding. He does it brilliantly well, in fact, by creating products that he then made iconic, like the hats with his campaign slogan on them. These create a sense of belonging. They are a uniform for his supporters to proudly display their team affiliation. Even so, crowdfunding is not the hallmark of his campaign in the public mind and comparatively irrelevant in comparison to the sheer volume of his personal wealth.

The public pledge Donald Trump has made to not take any donor money combined with his personal wealth ensures, to a degree, that he is not one of the globalist optimates that the populares are in revolt against. It creates a wall between him and them. Spending your own money and effort on something ensures that you are invested in seeing it work and are less likely to give up on it, so all of this is indicative of a degree of attachment to the popular revolt on the part of Donald Trump, pivoting his brand to its success.

Bernie Sanders does not have these luxuries. However, he has mastered the art of crowdfunding, raising enough money through small donations averaging $27 to be competitive with the Clinton political machine. As with Donald Trump, he has spoken against the *Citizens United* decision and disavowed SuperPACs (even though many are operating on his behalf). Bernie Sanders has explicitly called for a popular revolt by saying that "millions need to stand up" and assert themselves against "establishment politics and economics." His system of fundraising, or the one he's known for, rather, is reflective of that.

By sourcing his power from the grassroots, Bernie Sanders creates a separation between himself and the big donors, giving him credibility as a leader of the populares. Though the lack of a huge net worth like Donald Trump's makes his funding more difficult, it also ties his fortunes more closely to the people themselves, giving those who donate to him a sense of involvement in the campaign. Rather than merely spending his own money or rushing to raise money for SuperPACs like traditional candidates have done, Bernie Sanders is dependant on the people. It helps with the trust factor and dispelling lingering doubts among them, which Donald Trump's personal fortune leaves somewhat uncertain. It's all too easy to go back on your word after spending an inconsequential sum of your own money, after all. What's a few tens of millions (thus far, anyway) out of a fortune worth billions?

The ascendancy of alternative fundraising in politics, whether through sheer personal wealth or through crowdfunding, is changing the game, making populist rebellions more effective and enduring.

As the means of raising money become more diffuse, as the Bernie Sanders campaign has displayed so spectacularly in this election cycle, donor money is now worth less overall, for other games are in town. Why take it when you can find alternative means of raising money independently? Through this election cycle, the effectiveness of big donor money and SuperPACs has been disappearing.

Money is only a means to an end though. In politics, that capital is sunk into conducting the tactics and operations laid out in the previous chapters, and from there, building a winning coalition on the strategic level. Money is a gateway to the means of communication, of building a brand, building authority, establishing a media presence, denigrating opponents, and so on. Also crucial is spending that capital to put your infrastructure in place as a candidate such as paying your staff and for your ground game to get out the vote. These things are all greatly enhanced by something that is making donor money even less effective - the rise of a decentralized media apparatus.

Diffuse Communications:

Television ads, radio ads, and so on, the primary means of electioneering over the past half century, are expensive. Staff and ground operations are expensive. It's costly for a candidate to find a voice. It takes money, a lot of money, to reach the necessary market to build an electoral coalition.

Carl Sagan remarked in an interview with Ted Turner in 1989 (which was included in a video release of his groundbreaking 1980 *Cosmos* series) that "newspapers tend to propagate the view of the rich and powerful."[57]

One of the reasons for the failure of populist revolts in past decades, such as those spearheaded by Ross Perot, Pat Buchanan, and Ron Paul in far more recent times, is the fact that the media was concentrated in the hands of a few. Those few tended to have a distinct point of view, one which favored the globalist faction, the optimates, who needed to be appeased in order to play the political game.

But in 2016, things are different. As seen in chapters 5 and 6, the game is changing. The traditional mass media is losing money and viewership. If he were still alive today, Carl Sagan would be immensely pleased with the democratizing power of the internet and social media. For perhaps the first time in history, it is not necessary to own a significant amount of capital to distribute your message to a massive audience. The competition level has been raised by the lower barriers to entry, but anyone can now build a brand. Anyone can become an authority. It is now within the individual's power to make his own brand and define his own voice. News is percolating through a worldwide word-of-mouth network rather than being dictated from top-down gatekeepers.

The Cologne attacks on New Years' may have been covered up in years' past (as the Rotherham sexual violence was), but the door was blown wide open by word-of-mouth on social media. The people made the news instead of having it dictated to them. The police are now far more scrutinized because everyone has a high quality camera in the form of a phone, the contents of which can then be uploaded to the internet and spread like wildfire.

People are creating their own media outlets and talking amongst each other without established filters like never before, bringing issues to the fore from a point of view that had not, or could not, be widely expressed before. Issues that previously were ignored are now not only being spoken about, but have staying power. They are spreading through the ether and inciting people to rally around new ideas and worldviews that had not been widely disseminated in political circles previously. This network allows for the formation of new coalitions ready to play for power. It's a big reason why the "social justice warriors" became so prominent.

To make a long story short, the influence of DC talking heads and New York media studios is waning. The influence of independent, self-published media crafters and networks of unconnected individuals – standalone complexes, is on the rise.

These diffuse communications have allowed the Popular Revolt of 2016 to sustain itself and grow in power. Donald Trump and Bernie Sanders have been able to use the crowd on social media to distribute their message for them. This not only allows them to advertise, it also builds up their social proof, the most effective form of advertising, at much lower cost than traditional media ads.

The diffusion of communications also ties in perfectly with crowdfunding. As independent film and game makers use crowdfunding sites to raise money for their own projects which allow them to bypass the major studios, money from the populares can flow to new candidates to tackle new issues via internet communications and an online presence. It is no longer strictly necessary to go beg donor networks for money, but instead, candidates can take their message directly to the people through the internet and receive funding from sympathetic ears while building a network, consciously or not, of unrelated individuals to spread their message. In fact, candidates do not even need the donor money to reach those eyes and ears. Donald Trump can tweet or make Instagram videos for free. Bernie Sanders' enthusiastic supporters will gladly make YouTube videos for him free of charge.

This is all the latest iteration of the democratization of communications, and with them, political power.

In the past, only a few scribes under close supervision of the king and other high state officials knew how to read and write. The hieroglyphs and systems like Linear B or Cuneiform took highly professionalized training to understand.

When the easier to understand alphabet came along, there was a concurrent rise in independent cities, democracies, and republics. Through institutions like the Athenian Assembly and Rome's Twelve Tables, the rule of law became enshrined. Enough people were literate to know the law and hold everyone, including the rulers of the states, accountable to it.

When reading and writing became democratized with printing, the Protestant Reformation arose and spread.

When the telegraph, photography, telephone, radio, and motion pictures were invented, leaders were further held to account. Atrocities were harder to hide. The costs of war or other bad social policies were laid bare.

Each new communications revolution brings with it a concurrent sociopolitical revolution. This is what's happening now.

With the discontentment of the electorate very high, the means of communication diffuse, and with the concurrent and interconnected rise of new means of fundraising and self-promotion, all the necessary conditions were in place to create a populist revolt with staying power. The communications diffusion ensured that no hegemonic worldview would be dictated to the population from traditional gatekeepers. Information would instead spread from the grassroots. Those usually uncoordinated grassroots were now institutionalized and given enough power to challenge the optimate establishment.

Finally, the big issues that had been ignored for so long because of their benefitting the optimates would be extensively and critically examined by populare revolutionaries.

***

Takeaways:

1. Once more, it is imperative to be informed of the range of communication options available. Those who can take advantage of them, especially as new methods arise, will be the people with power. They will benefit both personally and professionally, as well as be in a commanding position to shape opinion and dictate events.

2. Take advantage of these diffuse communications to reach your key demographics and build your personal brand! It really is open season!

8. Someone Make Me an Offer!

This may have been the one phrase defining those who lived outside Georgetown, Manhattan, and Silicon Valley for decades. As mentioned in the previous chapter, dissatisfaction with traditional centrist parties of left and right, not just in the United States but indeed around the world, is extremely high. Distrust and disapproval of social institutions in government, business, and the media is also extremely high. For too long to too many, these institutions seemed to completely disregard them and their concerns, taking them for granted and expending them like pawns.

Finally, new grassroots institutions arose, and the people flocked to them. These disenfranchised people were only looking for someone to give them a voice. Donald Trump and Bernie Sanders answered.

One fundamental sales technique that has not been discussed in previous chapters has been the creation of offers. The best way to convert a prospect to a sale is to create a compelling offer. If no one wants what you're offering, or you have an idea rather than an offer, you will not sell. This is true even if you have all the other skills discussed so far. This is the major problem with the "establishment" candidates, especially in the Republican Party, this election cycle.

Donald Trump and Bernie Sanders created compelling offers because they actually talked about and pledged to solve the issues that people have in the forefront of their minds in one form or another. They offered solutions (or the ideas of solutions) to the **existential issues** that America is facing, the key concept of this chapter.

America facing "existential issues" doesn't refer to an apocalypse. It instead refers to the fact that if not solved; America will cease to exist as we currently know it. To some, that may be a good thing. To many others however, it is a deeply unsettling development, and this creates a yearning for someone to address the problem. Any offer to do so will be a powerful attraction to voters.

The previous chapter outlined the drive for globalization at any cost being the unifying thread between the elites, the optimates, in both parties. This is why nothing ever seems to really change where it counts between those two parties. The Democrats and Republicans will line up in opposition to each other over things like abortion, gay marriage, tax rates, specific regulations, and so on, but do you notice that on certain key issues relating to America's identity and place in the world, nothing ever seems to change?

Both Democratic and Republican elites strongly favor trade agreements like NAFTA. Recall that it was the first Bush administration that began negotiations on the deal and the Clinton administration that completed it. The Trans Pacific Partnership (TPP) began to be formulated under the second Bush administration. The Obama administration then did the major legwork on the negotiations, while Marco Rubio promised to finish the deal.

Marco Rubio's involvement with the "Gang of 8" 2013 Comprehensive Immigration Reform bill, which would have legalized the illegal immigrants living in the United States as well as increased legal immigration, is disdained by the Republican base. The bill was strongly supported by Barack Obama. Yet, recall that George W. Bush also backed the same kind of immigration reform during the middle of his second term in office when the Republican Party was at its most dominant position of power in decades.

While Barack Obama isn't as eager for full scale invasions as his predecessor, he nevertheless intervened in Libya and funneled weapons into Syria. He also threw his support behind the Arab Spring, which destabilized the Middle East and eventually set off the wave of migration currently convulsing Europe.

Meanwhile, political correctness based on identity politics has grown in power and morphed into the contemporary wave of "social justice warriors." While this is causing cognitive dissonance on the left, the establishment has supported it, as seen in both Hillary Clinton and even Bernie Sanders' campaigns. While the conservative movement has professed to oppose this, it has done so without success. It often doesn't even put up any opposition.

For the past few decades, under Democratic and Republican administrations alike, income inequality has grown. The economy has also grown, but little of that growth has benefitted those who don't own big assets. The richest people have made out like bandits while the middle class has shrunk dramatically. College degrees are often worthless and accrue lifetime indebtedness. Many, to quote a friend, "need to really be creative when it comes to making money." While anyone can now be their own entrepreneur through the diffusion of communications, this is still a difficult road, and it is not cut out for everyone. Some, perhaps most people, just need a good, stable job that pays the bills with some extra on the side. These jobs are now very difficult to find for wide segments of the population. The political center has failed to address this in any meaningful way, and to voters both left and right, it is a great betrayal.

This is the context in which the Popular Revolt of 2016 simmered, and the electorate instinctively knows that electing a Hillary Clinton or a Jeb Bush will not change the situation. On these issues, the existential issues – immigration (an issue which is transformative both economically and culturally), trade (and its effects on the fortunes of the working and middle classes as well as the sovereignty of America's Constitution and laws), foreign policy (an expensive and often disastrous endeavor under interventionist administrations, which spirals the debt and deficit and is often detrimental to international security, all the while threatening civil liberties here at home), and a culture of political correctness that seeks to control the very thoughts of the people, "to make windows into men's souls," to quote Elizabeth I, the leadership in both parties, big business, the media, and all the other traditional institutions, is in total agreement.

Therefore, the established candidates, the preferred choices of the optimates, could not create a compelling offer to wide segments and demographics of the American population that are dissatisfied with some or all of the above issues. The optimates all want to see the continuation of this status quo. Their offers may have been believed in the past, but the gates of influence have now been weakened. Alternative offers could be heard.

Why has Donald Trump failed to falter, and against all expectations, is poised to take the Republican Party's nomination? How come none of the optimates saw it coming? How come Donald Trump has had an almost limitless number of gaffes and outrages that would have killed anyone else in the past but emerges either unscathed or even stronger after each one? How come Bernie Sanders, a 74-year-old self-proclaimed socialist, in the face of a united establishment, is giving Hillary Clinton such a tough primary fight?

You've seen many of the answers in the preceding chapters, but the most fundamental one of all is that both Donald Trump and Bernie Sanders created very compelling offers to solve these issues, empowering those who have felt disenfranchised for decades. Their opponents were able to create no credible offers to fix these things. In fact, they usually aren't even mentioned at all. While Trump and Sanders offered benefits toward alleviating these existential issues, their opponents offered features related to things no one cares about. In short, no one is buying what they're selling anymore. The dismal performance of Marco Rubio, consistently the *strongest* of the GOP establishment candidates, and whose stances on the above issues marks himself as such, is the best evidence of this. Even Hillary Clinton has been forced to oppose the TPP, which she was a key figure in negotiating and which she called the "gold standard," because of Bernie Sanders' strong run. The offer of the establishment, especially in the Republican Party, is worthless.

This is the biggest reason why, again and again, Donald Trump has been able to survive and thrive after every damning confrontation. For all of his sales skills and his ability to attract the attention and retain the interests of his prospects, numerous objections may still remain. The offer must be good enough to overcome these logical objections. Does this contradict the hypothesis that human decision-making is mostly irrational? No, because the negative emotions associated with these existential issues will cause people to beg for a solution, even if it isn't the best one – just something, *anything*, and Donald Trump's offer is visceral and to the point.

Donald Trump's offer to build a wall on the border is both magnificent and visual. It is a wanted solution to a nagging problem that people have been complaining about for decades – illegal immigration.

Donald Trump's offer to reform immigration away from the current regime of mass family reunification and to end abuses in programs like the H1B visa was salivated over by people whose economic prospects have shrunk and who are uncomfortable with the forced cultural change of their communities and country.

Donald Trump's offer to reject and renegotiate trade deals that shuttered the industry of so many communities and left them destitute and drug-addicted was powerful.

Donald Trump's offer to stop wasteful foreign interventions was a rallying cry to all but the neoconservatives in the Republican Party, who have a terrible brand because of the second Bush administration and the war in Iraq.

Donald Trump's offer to blow the door down on political correctness, and with such a strong personal example, was inspiring to everyone. People finally felt brave enough to voice what they were secretly feeling but were too afraid to say.

Donald Trump went on to dominate the space on all of these issues, which so many Americans were frustrated about. Because of his actions as seen in the second chapter, he is often perceived as being the only game in town on all of them.

Why can't the "establishment" defeat Donald Trump? The fact that the establishment candidates all lack the other sales skills discussed so far is very important, but the most crucial reason is that the establishment, the optimates, cannot create a compelling counteroffer to Trump's to an electorate that is in the midst of rebellion, a rebellion which insulates Trump from any criticism. Those criticizing him – politicians, the media, all those within the optimate class, are not trusted. Their authority is negative. Worse, their increasingly desperate attacks on him have only further convinced his populare supporters, who hate the optimates, that he is their champion. They have turned him into a symbol of rebellion.

To the populares, Donald Trump is a symbol of rebellion against a corrupt and condescending political class.

To the populares, Donald Trump is a symbol of rebellion against a media apparatus that they find dishonest and slanderous.

To the populares, Donald Trump is a symbol of rebellion against the influx of migrants in their communities without their consent.

To the populares, Donald Trump is a symbol of rebellion against the disappearance of their livelihoods across the sea.

To the populares, Donald Trump is a symbol of rebellion against American imperialism that doesn't seem to benefit Americans.

To the populares, Donald Trump is a symbol of rebellion against the ever-intrusive thought policing of political correctness.

In other words, Donald Trump knew his market:

> I don't hire a lot of number-crunchers, and I don't trust fancy marketing surveys. I do my own surveys and draw my own conclusions. I'm a great believer in asking everyone for an opinion before I make a decision. It's a natural reflex. If I'm thinking of buying a piece of property, I'll ask the people who live nearby about the area – what they think of the schools and the crime and the shops. When I'm in another city and I take a cab, I'll always make it a

point to ask the cabdriver questions. I ask and I ask and I ask, until I begin to get a gut feeling about something. And that's when I make a decision.

I have learned much more from conducting my own random surveys than I could ever have learned from the greatest of consulting firms. They send a crew of people down from Boston, rent a room in New York, and charge you $100,000 for a lengthy study. In the end, it has no conclusion and takes so long to complete that if the deal you were considering was a good one, it will be long gone.

The other people I don't take too seriously are the critics – except when they stand in the way of my projects. In my opinion, they mostly write to impress each other, and they're just as swayed by fashions as anyone else. What very few of them have is any feeling for what the public wants.[58]

If the optimates had been able to, or will be able to, effectively attack Trump's offers and make counteroffers of their own, Trump would or will collapse. His symbol would lose some of its meaning. However, because he dominates so much space with his offers and has so much authority on them, this has not been possible. Worse, the people advising them usually fit into the above mold Trump lambasted in his *The Art of the Deal*. They hire expensive pollsters and form their opinions in their gated communities and beltway bubbles. How would they be able to create a compelling offer for the rest of America?

The only candidate in the race who has been able to make a somewhat effective counteroffer is Ted Cruz. As seen after Super Tuesday, Ted Cruz is offering the persona and record of a consistent, reliable conservative, compared to the supposedly stealth liberal, Donald Trump. These attacks have been effective, given Trump's slight subpar performance on what was called Super Saturday. He lost a state that he probably should have won – Maine, and won Louisiana and Kentucky by narrower margins than expected. As Marco Rubio collapsed in the lead up to and after Super Tuesday and Ben Carson dropped out of the race, it seemed that Cruz was consolidating a coalition of "true conservatives" (those voters who identify as "very conservative") and panicking optimates in the establishment to stop Trump.

Cruz's brand as a "true conservative who's stood up to Washington" and his offer of, namely, stopping Donald Trump, is compelling. Ted Cruz has not been able to dominate the space on the existential issues that many Americans feel that the country is facing – immigration, trade, foreign policy, but he has been able to use Trump's dominance against him and dominate the space of the "#NeverTrump" movement consisting of those who want to see Trump stopped at any cost. To them, Donald Trump is the existential issue facing the Republican Party and perhaps even the country itself.

In this way, Ted Cruz's brand and offer satisfies both a potent wing of the popular revolt against the globalist optimates in Washington (which is tired of nominating "RINOs") as well as some of those panicked globalists themselves who fear Trump. We do live in strange times.

A revolt on the right wing was inevitable. For decades, the conservative movement failed to oppose the left in a meaningful way in any of the social institutions, whether in politics, academia, the entertainment industry, or anywhere else. By its own definitions, as seen in the mission statement of *National Review*, the most influential publication of the conservative movement, it has failed spectacularly. Worse, when acolytes of that movement have actually held power, they have accelerated that which they were supposed to oppose.

In the second Bush administration, when conservatives had a decided upper hand, government expanded at its fastest pace since that hallmark of leftism, Lyndon Johnson. In all the existential issues, the optimates in the conservative movement betrayed the wishes of their own grassroots. The most common apology for the actions of the Bushes, the Romneys, the McCains, and so forth is that they aren't "true conservatives," but that is simply a No True Scotsman fallacy.

Many remark that the conservative movement is a dying beast and that it truly does not have much support:

> What so frightens the conservative movement about Trump's success is that he reveals just how thin the support for their ideas really is. His campaign is a rebuke to their institutions. It says the Republican Party doesn't need all these think tanks, all this supposed policy expertise. It says look at these people calling themselves libertarians and conservatives, the ones in tassel-loafers and bow ties. Have they made you more free? Have their endless policy papers and studies and books conserved anything for you? These people are worthless. They are defunct. You don't need them, and you're better off without them.[59]

Donald Trump's offers gave the popular revolt on the right exactly what it wanted to buy – an alternative to the optimates and a conservative movement that seemed out of touch with itself at best and uncaring toward the people at worst, betraying its own voters and insulting and denigrating them when challenged. Mitt Romney and John McCain's recent actions denouncing Trump confirmed this to all too many. Trump researched this massive and growing market and projected his offer accordingly. The establishment, believing that the revolt would only be a minor brushfire as in years' past, did not do the proper research and could not make an appropriate offer. Instead, the optimates went into battle first and then sought victory.

***

Takeaways:

1. Whatever it is you're doing, know your market or your entire grand plan is worthless. Do not isolate yourself from that market with consultants or focus groups that will charge you too much money. Instead, mine the internet, social media, forums, etc. Become part of the communities you seek to sell to. Talk to everyone. Make use of tools like keyword trackers or very specific targeted ads, such as those on Facebook. Google Trends is also very useful in spotting growth markets around keywords and phrases. Remember that connection is an integral part of charisma. Build trust and authority with those communities.

2. After having mined and participated in your marketplace, make a compelling offer to fulfill its desires or assuage its fears and problems, one that you're confident it will want to buy, while remembering the techniques discussed so far to spruce it up.

9. The Pendulum Will Swing

I don't spend all of my time analyzing politics, current events, and salesmanship. Like most people, I have my own indulgent, seemingly meaningless hobbies. One of these is analyzing the hypothetical outcome of "versus battles" that usually involve fictional characters. Think Goku from Dragon Ball Z vs. Superman, though humorously, that matchup is currently banned at the forum where I do this.

I actually don't do many of these debates anymore. I had a few good years of debating intensely. I now return mainly for the community and to scale it upward as a business due to our successful web database, outskirtsbattledomewiki.com.

The guys there are interesting. They're certainly not politically correct. Slurs of all kinds are often used as terms of endearment. Still, many of them were supporting Obama in 2012. Mitt Romney was widely despised and mocked as "Mittens." On the day that he lost so decisively to Barack Obama, I recall one of the regulars saying that "maybe the Republicans would have won if they didn't pick an insane bigot as their candidate."

Four years later, just before I started writing this book, that same community and even that same member is speaking highly of Donald Trump. They certainly admire his brash and unapologetic attitude and "how salty he makes people," in that member's own words.

That was another sign to me that Donald Trump would win.

The community there is far less political than I am. They're normal guys talking about normal stuff. Donald Trump certainly has more credibility of being an "insane bigot" than Mitt Romney in the public's mind. Yet, he's spoken of highly in that same community by that same member. How could this possibly be?

In politics, it's understood that there is generally a pendulum. Periods of left-of-center rule are followed by periods of right-of-center rule and then back again. In American history, this has been seen in both shorter cycles in differing elections, where one party replaces another, and in longer cycles where one party has tended to dominate most of the elections in a particular period or party system, such as the Republican Party's dominance from Reconstruction to the Great Depression, and then the Democratic Party's prominence from the Great Depression until 1968.

Old ideas get stale. The crucial demographics of power that can shift elections grow tired of one party and decide to "throw the rascals out" in favor of the other party. The election of Barack Obama was just as much a repudiation of George W. Bush as it was a vote of confidence in the former.

Perhaps the infamous "second term curse," the curious fact of history that second presidential terms are often tougher for their occupants than their first, has something to do with the tiring. George W. Bush's second term saw him faced with numerous and terrible difficulties. It presented the Iraq quagmire for all it was worth, Hurricane Katrina, and the financial collapse of 2008. These are certainly in large part to blame for the quick sinking of his fortunes among the people.

To give Barack Obama credit, his second term has faced none of these catastrophes thus far and with little to go. This does indeed reflect in his overall approval rating as of the time of this writing, which is much healthier than Bush's was at the same point in his own presidency. While the rise of ISIS and continued stark income inequality are far from positive, these issues aren't the firebombs that exploded the latter days of the Bush administration.

Yet Obama's second term did yield a cultural phenomenon that left a sour taste in the mouths of a growing number of people. This was the rise of the "social justice warrior."

Everything in the past few years seems to be "triggering" to someone. Outrage has replaced baseball as the national pastime, it seems. Harvard recently abolished the word "master" in titles because of some supposed link to racism and slavery. In early 2015, a college refused to perform the feminist classic *The Vagina Monologues* in an annual recital because it "wasn't inclusive enough, since not all women have vaginas." Members of the military have been forced to wear high heels and "walk a mile in her shoes." More ominously, there has been the scalping of individuals like Brendan Eich, creator of Javascript. In 2014, he was forced to leave his job as CEO of Mozilla after a pressure campaign over his small donation to a pro-traditional marriage group in California in 2008. In recent years, political correctness has become omnipresent in daily life. Most Americans now consider this a major problem.

The rise of the social justice warriors is a large reason for the current preference falsifications discussed in chapter 5, and while this all may be popular with academia, Hollywood, and campus activists, especially on social media, it is stifling and infuriating to the overwhelming majority of the population. While relatively quiet in his first term on issues such as these, Barack Obama has coddled the social justice warriors at every turn in his second term. Ranging from dubious campus rape outrages to race-baiting controversies, the president gave his approval to nearly any social justice warrior endeavor. This did bleed over into the government.

Hillary Clinton has tried to pander hard to young Millennial social justice warriors in her campaign. Her opening advertisement in April 2015 was homage to every "social justice" identity group imaginable. Yet, despite her attempts to reach out to this group, they have often backfired, as seen in the "#NotMyAbuela" boondoggle in the latter stages of 2015.

This distinctly left wing virtue signaling and the cultural shifts it has wrought has tired many people, who think that it has gone too far. It's gone far enough, and has gotten absurd enough, that many on the political left are also alienated.

In this atmosphere, where people increasingly feel their voices being stifled and are annoyed by what they see as an infestation of sanctimonious social justice warriors into every aspect of their lives, Donald Trump offered them an outlet. As the pendulum swung so far to the left, Donald Trump was the equal and opposite reaction. The existential issues outlined in the previous chapter may have been the powder waiting to be ignited, but the social justice warriors were the primer. They contributed to the pendulum swing which will ultimately reckon with these issues when it moves rightward. Indeed, these issues were made worse by the fact that the social justice warriors were another force preventing them from being addressed.

Suddenly, Donald Trump seems less an "insane bigot" than Mitt Romney, because people are now tired of social justice warriors and their omnipresent outrages. In an age where everything is "racist" or in some other way bigoted, in truth, nothing is bigoted, because the denigrating label has been diluted to meaninglessness. The usual labels simply don't have the power they did four years ago.

Explore the pendulum phenomenon and you will see the change in party dominance over a number of election cycles. In the modern era (post-World War II), White House occupancy has changed hands constantly between the parties. After eight-year spans in power or even sooner, the White House has swapped. The only party to hold three consecutive presidential terms since World War II was the Republican Party from 1981-1993. The reaction to that was to elect Bill Clinton and usher in an era of Democratic dominance in the popular vote in presidential contests (though were it not for Ross Perot, George H.W. Bush would have likely won in 1992 – politics is always a tricky business).

Yet, there is perhaps another, unexamined phenomenon at work.

The natural dissatisfaction with the Republican George W. Bush was to elect the Democrat Barack Obama. This did not mean that overall satisfaction with the Democratic Party among the American people at large improved, it just meant that it was the grudging alternative. Many were hoping for change, but did not get it, for reasons already explained. In a revolting electorate, the standard two party pendulum swing is no longer good enough. There is now a third dimension or perhaps even a fourth when you consider the previous discussion about party dominance over the long term in what are known as party systems amongst political scientists.

In an electorate that wants change from globalization at any cost, whether consciously knowing this or not, the pendulum was also set far enough to blow back on traditional optimate politics. Throughout history, periods of globalization have then been followed by periods of retrenchment. This is the fourth dimension of the pendulum. For example, the 19th century, following the defeat of Napoleon, was generally a period of globalization. World War I ended it.

Ultimately, both Donald Trump and Bernie Sanders are forces indicating that the pendulum on the latest period of globalization is swinging back, though the troubles in the European Union and elsewhere are also indicative. The rebellious forces in the Democratic Party, the populares, are probably not going to succeed this time, just as other rebellious forces elsewhere haven't succeeded yet, but their strength is growing.

Donald Trump is a reaction to both the latest period of globalization and the ascendancy of the left in "social justice" culture which was made particularly obvious in Barack Obama's second term.

Unlike the Roman optimates, today's elite class is composed of globalists in the true sense of the word. In the eyes of the populares, they are seen as having no loyalty to their people or any nation, only to money and the dictates of the various branches of their Universalist liberal (small "l"), globalist, ivory tower ideology. The distrust and disdain they have sown amongst the populace toward them and the social institutions that glue society together can never be good things, and this creates the clamoring for a strongman to solve the problems. The stage is set almost perfectly for a Donald Trump triumph. Donald Trump has constantly admonished the leadership that so many people perceive as incompetent and out of touch, so the question arises – why continue listening to them?[60]

This is perhaps even a fifth dimension of the pendulum, one which swings from weak to strong leaders. This makes the things the optimates have done and continue to do especially dangerous.

Despite the media hysterics, Donald Trump is no Hitler or Mussolini, but his style is more authoritarian than others, in part because of his mastery of the mechanisms of influence that previous chapters have explored. Trump is seen by many as a messy, but appropriate outlet, but I fear that the pendulum will be even more over-reactive if the optimates continue to tug it in the wrong, unpopular direction.

***

Takeaways:

1. Every action has an equal and opposite reaction. This is as true in social phenomena as it is in physics.

2. Those who can take advantage of the coming reaction will be able to profit immensely if they make the right offer as part of the pendulum swing. This is almost a heavenly gift, as your offer and attempts at influence will almost create themselves should you recognize it.

3. To find the reaction, you must do what Donald Trump advised in *The Art of the Deal*. Talk to everyone on the ground and online. Embed innocent, noncommittal quips on social or political phenomena in conversations with friends or even strangers to get an idea of what people really think about things. On other topics, see if there is a coming reaction against the latest fad involving your key demographic. See if there are rumblings of a new fad that challenges the wisdom of the older one. Probe social media, internet forums, search engine data, and other outlets to find where the trends are going. When you have a general idea, learn more and create a product designed for the pendulum swing, much like this very book.

10. The Don of Uncertainty

Donald Trump is undoubtedly a wild card. His management and overall style, for one, is unstructured, as he explains in *The Art of the Deal*:

> Most people are surprised by the way I work. I play it very loose. I don't carry a briefcase. I try not to schedule too many meetings. I leave my door open. You can't be imaginative or entrepreneurial if you've got too much structure. I prefer to come to work each day and just see what develops.[61]

He also likes to tout his unpredictability factor, mentioning that it has helped him in business to secure his projects.[62] On the campaign trail, he's declared that America's leadership is too predictable, which in turn hampers the fight against dangerous enemies like ISIS.

Humans are naturally risk-averse. The familiar is pleasant, the fear of change real. Under normal conditions, a Donald Trump candidacy would be a flash in the pan upon realization of this fact by the multitude because of his unpredictability and the fear it creates, alongside the fear many have of him by default. However, as we've seen, this is a deeply abnormal election cycle. The populace is in revolt and clamoring for change, and not just in party, but in a deep, meaningful way. The pendulum is swinging in multiple directions instead of just one. That's why so few are buying the traditional offers of the optimates.

Donald Trump may be a wild card. No one seems to know what his real intentions truly are. However, he is talking about and dominating the space on the existential issues related to globalization that broad swathes of the American populace are growing tired of – the current immigration, trade, and foreign policy doctrines, as well as political correctness that swung the pendulum so far to the left, particularly during the second term of the Obama administration. All of these issues have not only remained unaddressed, but the ivory tower condescends, tars, and even attempts to ruin the lives of those who try to come to terms with them.

This creates, quite frankly, a situation of desperation. With so many Americans living in debt with zero or underwater assets, unable to find a job that pays the bills, tired of seeing their communities and culture being changed by, to them, excessive immigration, tired of seeing wasteful foreign adventures, and tired of being silenced by political correctness, they are looking for someone, anyone, to alleviate those concerns. Any offer to do so will be responded to with enthusiasm, especially when done with as much marketing savvy as Trump has done in his campaign.

Under normal circumstances, if another, less wild candidate with a bit of marketing savvy had been able to make a similar offer, Trump would have likely collapsed, but as mentioned before, the other offers simply aren't believable.

People will take Trump because to them, it cannot get worse than it is now. They will hold out hope for something better rather than doing more of the same that has, in their eyes, failed them so miserably. The field was wide open for Trump to dominate space, even without exerting much effort on his own part, and that's exactly what he did. Trump saw such a situation and acted.

Recently, Jim Webb, a former Democratic senator from Virginia who had taken a long shot at the party's nomination and failed, mentioned that he would not be voting for Hillary Clinton because of her foreign policy history. He did however, not rule out an endorsement and vote for Donald Trump, saying that his potential presidency could be something either very good or very bad.

For many, especially Trump's supporters, the feeling is that with Donald Trump, you may not know what you're getting, but with everyone else, you do. With Trump, you may get played, but with the usual candidates, *you know you're getting played.* Donald Trump, of course, does everything to promote this fact, constantly denigrating politicians, calling them "all talk, no action" people who serve their "lobbyists, special interests, and donors." It's a message of big merit to an electorate in revolt.

If the choice is between an uncertain character who offers change from a hated regime with no alternatives and a certain one who will bring more of the same policies that are found to be revolting, people will opt to take the risk and go with the uncertain character.

This is why questions over Donald Trump's temperament, sincerity, and other embarrassments from his past never get to him. His offer is too good to pass up and many voters will take risks to see it pay off.

***

Takeaway:

Human beings will usually not take risks unless they must. If you find a market that is desperately seeking change and can provide convincing solutions, they may be very happy indeed to take that risk with you. They may also be likely to defend you when you're attacked because they want a solution so badly. Impulsive action will be extremely strong in this scenario – which is exactly what you want.

11. The Realigning Election of 2016

Donald Trump's tactics (domination of issues and opponents with his iron frame), operations (his charisma, mastery of crowd psychology, his personal brand), and the largest part of his strategy (his offer and the context in which it is made) have now been explained. The next crucial question is how he ties it all together. How does he leverage all of this into electoral victory?

Every so often in American history, there is what many political scientists call a realigning election. In these elections, new electoral coalitions arise to deal with new issues which supersede the old ones in prominence, new methods of campaigning are often introduced, and generally a new political zeitgeist is formed for the coming era. One party may rise to dominance at the expense of the other in this process as they shift their general platforms to take on the new issues.

Those precise elections that can be said to be distinctly realigning is a subject of heated debate. Generally however, there is widespread agreement that these six elections were realigning ones: 1800, 1828, 1860, 1896, 1932, and 1968. It is interesting that a common characteristic of all of these elections is that they were particularly nasty in their tone and occurred in years of widespread social controversy which deeply divided the nation and electorate. They were the staunchest witnesses to the warnings that George Washington gave in his 1796 farewell address on the dangers of partisan politics:

> I have already intimated to you the danger of parties in the State, with particular reference to the founding of them on geographical discriminations. Let me now take a more comprehensive view, and warn you in the most solemn manner against the baneful effects of the spirit of party generally.

> This spirit, unfortunately, is inseparable from our nature, having its root in the strongest passions of the human mind. It exists under different shapes in all governments, more or less stifled, controlled, or repressed; but, in those of the popular form, it is seen in its greatest rankness, and is truly their worst enemy.

The alternate domination of one faction over another, sharpened by the spirit of revenge, natural to party dissension, which in different ages and countries has perpetrated the most horrid enormities, is itself a frightful despotism. But this leads at length to a more formal and permanent despotism. The disorders and miseries which result gradually incline the minds of men to seek security and repose in the absolute power of an individual; and sooner or later the chief of some prevailing faction, more able or more fortunate than his competitors, turns this disposition to the purposes of his own elevation, on the ruins of public liberty.

Without looking forward to an extremity of this kind (which nevertheless ought not to be entirely out of sight), the common and continual mischiefs of the spirit of party are sufficient to make it the interest and duty of a wise people to discourage and restrain it.

It serves always to distract the public councils and enfeeble the public administration. It agitates the community with ill-founded jealousies and false alarms, kindles the animosity of one part against another, foments occasionally riot and insurrection. It opens the door to foreign influence and corruption, which finds a facilitated access to the government itself through the channels of party passions. Thus the policy and the will of one country are subjected to the policy and will of another.

There is an opinion that parties in free countries are useful checks upon the administration of the government and serve to keep alive the spirit of liberty. This within certain limits is probably true; and in governments of a monarchical cast, patriotism may look with indulgence, if not with favor, upon the spirit of party. But in those of the popular character, in governments purely elective, it is a spirit not to be encouraged. From their natural tendency, it is certain there will always be enough of that spirit for every salutary purpose. And there being constant danger of excess, the effort ought to be by force of public opinion, to mitigate and assuage it. A fire not to be quenched, it demands a uniform vigilance to prevent its bursting into a flame, lest, instead of warming, it should consume.[63]

Indeed, strongmen that Washington would likely have been wary of have often seemed to emerge in the aftermath of these realigning elections. The world, when ready, is dragged kicking and screaming into those new eras by such strong, dynamic personalities. Arguably, Washington was one himself, much as he may have detested such a label.

What's perhaps even more interesting about these realigning elections is that they have occurred with an almost mechanical degree of regularity. Look closely and you will find the following trend:

1800 > 28-year-span > 1828 > 32-year-span > 1860 > 36-year-span > 1896 > 36-year-span > 1932 > 36-year-span > 1968.

If you add up all the time spans between these widely-cited realigning elections and get an average, you'll find one of 33.6 years. In other words, there has generally been a realigning election once a generation in American history. Upon looking at it this way, you may realize that technically the country is overdue for a realigning election by over a decade. It's been 48 years since the last one. Why is there currently a popular revolt brewing in both parties? It's because both parties are stale. No one buys what they're selling anymore. The people want new offers from both brands. Trump is making such an offer in the Republican Party and Bernie Sanders is in the Democratic Party.

When partisan politics get stale, new political markets are formed, and ultimately the parties will have to serve those new markets in order to continue to win elections. These new political price signals are communicated through realigning elections. The market shifts and offers are made for a new era of the political marketplace.

While some dispute the theory of realignment altogether, it is nevertheless useful, especially when looking at the current makeup of the Republican Party and how it is now being undone at the seams.

The American system is distinctly unfavorable to more than two parties. Because of this, the Democratic and Republican Parties function as very big tents, whereas in other countries with parliamentary systems, the different wings in each party would probably have their own separate parties. In a Republican Party that's produced a number of insurgencies and insurgent candidates over the past few election cycles, and with dissatisfaction of the party's elite amongst its base high, with failure and betrayal for decades, a turnover in the party's directions, a realignment, was inevitable. The only thing up in the air was what direction that realignment would take.

To ponder that question, it's necessary to take a look at the major factions within the tent of the Republican Party. The original survey came from a surprisingly nuanced article from CNBC, a survey which is here expanded.[64] Essentially, there are three major factions which make up the big tent:

Globalists: These are the optimates in the party – think the Bushes, John McCain, and Mitt Romney. They're the ones you'll find in government, academia, in the conservative think tanks, and at publications like the *Wall Street Journal*, *National Review*, and the *Weekly Standard*. Their numbers are actually small, but their influence is enormous. As their name implies, their focus is on globalization. They support open borders and mass immigration, neoliberal trade deals like NAFTA, and foreign interventions like the invasion of Iraq. In the latter, they are motivated by Wilsonian internationalism, as seen when George W. Bush thought the country would seamlessly transition into democracy. They claim to stand up to political correctness but don't do much of it in practice, and if the recent "#NeverTrump" campaign is any indication, they co-opt the pathology for their own purposes. Neoconservatism and the Israel lobby are strong influences among them. They also have an axiomatic belief in tax cuts and the free market. In that regard (the economic realm), libertarianism is a strong influence. Late in the primary cycle, Marco Rubio emerged as the champion of this faction, though his fortunes still faded fast.

Religious Right: These are the moral majority people. Think of Rick Santorum, Mike Huckabee, the Falwells of the world, and so on. Their power structure is less organized, but still formidable, comprising groups such as Focus on the Family. While their influence is declining, they nevertheless still hold considerable space in the Republican narrative, as seen in the fact that it's imperative to denounce abortion and gay marriage in Republican primaries. These social issues – abortion, gay marriage, stem cell research, and so on, are this faction's calling card. The Israel lobby is a strong influence with this group as well, since many evangelicals believe it to be of eschatological significance. Though subordinate to the globalist optimates, they are in fact the junior governing partner in the Republican electoral coalition, as seen by the prominence that their issues get. This wing, comprised significantly of evangelical Christians, has large amounts of voters, as seen in the success of its current champion, Ted Cruz.

Nationalists: Donald Trump's core base. His success in such a wide number of demographics and across states that differ as much as Georgia and Massachusetts signifies that this is probably the single largest faction within the Republican Party, though it has also been to this point the most disorganized.

Largely American traditionalists, they are protective of their culture and way of life. They are typically averse to government power and expansion, but not to the point of ideological axiom like libertarians, and see some role for government to ensure the well-being of the people and nation (for example: programs like Medicare, Medicaid, and Social Security tend to be popular with this group). They want a strong America, but not an imperial one that plays the role of policeman of the world. In that regard, libertarian foreign policy is generally influential. As they are protective of their nation, people, and culture, they oppose mass immigration and neoliberal trade deals like NAFTA, which ship their jobs overseas and are to them, intolerable breaches of the country's sovereignty. This group has not had much formal representation, but it has started to coalesce through the power of the diffusion of media. In the Popular Revolt of 2016, it is surging with a vengeance. These are the populares.

When going over this census, don't take these groups as being always and everywhere mutually exclusive. Most people will probably be a mixture of two. Some might be a mixture of all three. This is the place where logic finally comes into play and where the ivory tower gets its grudging due. People will generally have a preference structure of issues, for whatever reason, logical or not, and spend their vote accordingly…or at least they think they have one, until something in the moment disrupts this logic and causes them to make a different decision than they had originally thought they would make.

The status quo in Republican politics had its beginnings in Richard Nixon's 1968 campaign. Since then, the dominant issues in the Republican Party have largely been globalist ones with social issues given secondary prominence. Yet, throughout the most recent decades, there have been signs of a nascent nationalist, or perhaps more accurately, nationalist-based/prioritized uprising. This was seen in the candidacies of Ross Perot, Pat Buchanan, and Ron Paul. These campaigns had surprising levels of support. Yet, they were unable to advance beyond the first phase. In the case of the former two, the time was not yet right. The issues related to globalization were not yet advanced enough to form a critical mass of rebellious voters, the media was not decentralized enough, and these first rebel leaders did not possess the skills that have been outlined in previous chapters. There was simply not an impetus big enough to resist and realign the Republican Party's elites.

In the case of Ron Paul, the time was close, but still not quite there. The results of globalist policies were clear, yet the media was still not decentralized enough, even in 2012, to mount a truly effective insurgent campaign. The gatekeepers still held on to enough power to prevent it. Ron Paul did not possess the skills that have been outlined in this book, and his purist libertarianism didn't do him any favors.

Yet, 2016 is different. The nationalist faction has been able to organize and communicate effectively with the decentralization of media. With the right champion, the populares are now poised to overrun the optimates and realign Republican Party politics away from globalism with a minority focus on social issues toward a relatively free market, "common sense conservative," nationalist party with shades of Andrew Jackson and Theodore Roosevelt. The new Republican Party may be one which is suspicious of both big government and crony capitalism, but is also desirous that government should act in the interests of the American people, not exclusively to corporations or to an abstract, globalized world. The axiomatic stances toward tax cuts and regulations may end (in fact, the Republican base is far from as axiomatic over these as the optimates are).[65] Instead of a priori opposition to either, the new Republican Party may be one which asks whether they are needed, limited, and above all, smart. There may also be a "Trump Doctrine" version of Roosevelt's "big stick diplomacy," a foreign policy based exclusively on national interests, instead of neoconservative interventionism.

This is essentially the offer that Trump is making to an electorate in revolt. Who does he, partially through his sales techniques, get to buy it? He has his core of nationalist Republicans firmly in his tent, but this will not be enough to win a general election. What electoral coalition may form out of this 2016 Republican realignment to dominate rightist politics for the next few decades?

The first and most obvious place to look is the religious right, the current junior partner in the Republican governing coalition. They are just as dissatisfied with the globalist optimates in the Republican Party as the nationalist-centered faction, perhaps for similar but not entirely identical reasons. Abortion has not been made illegal. Gay marriage has been made legal. What they perceive as cultural decay has certainly accelerated. The new nationalist drive will likely largely turn away from these as motivating issues, as Trump tends to dodge them with success (but not always). Even so, most of this faction will find the Republican nationalist brand superior to the Democrats in a general election. Aside from that, the tribal nature of voting, where party affiliation and past voting behavior matter above all else, should swing nearly all of this faction to Trump in a general election.

Some of the Republican establishment optimates in the globalist faction will bolt. Yet, their numbers are small enough so as not to make a huge difference. This was seen very clearly in Virginia, where Marco Rubio only won the northern portion nearest Washington, and in Florida, where he only won the Miami area. Before dropping out, he only won one small state, Minnesota.

Some of these voters will probably come around begrudgingly, as their behavior of voting Republican is institutionalized. People trust and repeat the familiar. The cudgel of the Supreme Court up for grabs, wielded by Trump at his press conference on Super Saturday, was brilliant.

Yet this is taken for granted, and it will still not be enough to win a general election. Trump will need crossover voting demographics – independents and others. To examine the full extent of Trump's strategy, the realigning electoral coalition that may build around him, it's necessary to zoom out further on the map and take a look at the Democratic Party's tent. It also comprises three major factions.

Globalists: These are the Clintons, Barack Obama, and so on. While they don't have an axiomatic belief in tax cuts like their Republican counterparts and may differ on a few things like the degree of foreign adventurism, they are essentially no different from their supposed opponents in the conservative movement. They favor mass immigration, neoliberal trade deals, and are keen to intervene in foreign entanglements.

Social Justice Warriors: The junior governing partner in the Democratic coalition. They are the dominant force in academia. They are akin to the religious right, as they have a deep, zealous conviction in their beliefs – identity politics. Unlike the religious right, however, they have been in the ascendant. They are younger than average. Hillary Clinton has attempted to pander to them, though usually unsuccessfully.

Old School Liberals: In some ways these are the intellectual descendants (though not the mirror images) of the New Deal Coalition that fell apart in the late 60's culminating in the realigning election of 1968. They are concerned about civil rights issues, but are growing increasingly skeptical of the identity politics of social justice warriors. They have a nationalistic streak and have largely been disorganized and shut out, particularly since Bill Clinton and the New Left came to power. Their major concerns are questions of fairness for the American working and middle classes. They typically oppose neoliberal trade deals like NAFTA and the TPP as well as foreign adventurism. Opinions vary on immigration. The focus is on economic over more essentialist considerations as seen with the social justice warriors. Jim Webb is one of these, but Bernie Sanders is obviously the current champion of this faction.

When looking at the old school liberals and Trump's core, Republican nationalist base, do you see anything similar? Moreover, have you noticed any similarities between Trump's and Sanders' campaigns if you can cut through the bombast?

You'd find an audience receptive to similar offers. Both campaigns are running against neoliberal trade deals and interventionist foreign policy. Both campaigns have dominated the space of these existential issues in their respective primary fields. This creates the potential for crossovers.

A revealing poll came out a few months ago that suggested that in a Trump/Clinton general election, as many as 20% of Democrats could cross over to vote for Trump.[66] This was of course, only one poll and at a very remote time from Election Day. Nevertheless, it was revealing. If anything close to that occurs, the election would be over.

Who comprises that 20%? The probable answer is that it's a large portion of the Bernie Sanders or Jim Webb Democrats – those who are frustrated that the Party seems to have turned its back on the working and middle class population it is supposed to champion in favor of globalism and identity politics. Jim Webb's remarks, highlighted earlier, are indicative of the general unpopularity of Hillary Clinton with many Democrats. They also indicate how Trump's offer may be more appealing. It's an offer he can certainly promote to this strategic group of voters with his salesmanship.

The Democratic base can be carved further into more distinct demographics. Which of these may support Trump?

White Democrats: As seen, once more, in Jim Webb. Given Hillary Clinton's very poor performance with white men in the Democratic primaries thus far and Bernie Sanders' winning states with very large white population percentages, this is a core group that may find Donald Trump more appealing. The party, under the influence of social justice warriors and identity politics, may just alienate more whites, especially white men, with what they may see as blatant pandering to minorities at their expense. It may just drive what remains of white voters, especially in the working and middle class, into Trump's hands. Furthermore, given the continued distress of much of this group due to globalization, particularly in the Rust Belt, an offer akin to Trump's - of alleviating those pressures by opposing unpopular trade deals - could bring a crucial portion over. This possibility was seen in Bernie Sanders' huge upset win in Michigan when the polls had him down by 20 points. He hammered Hillary Clinton over trade. As such, Michigan Democrats narrowly chose him. More tellingly, over 20,000 Democrats left the party in recent months to become independents or Republicans in Massachusetts, where Trump won its mixed primary (where both independents and Republicans could vote) by 49%. The same indications are also shaping up to be true in Pennsylvania, where 46,000 Democrats have switched their affiliation to Republican.[67]

Black Voters: Democrats have relied on the black vote for the past fifty years. Yet, despite the gains in civil rights, the black community has also fallen on hard times. Their families have fallen apart, their sons mass incarcerated, their prospects shrunken. Because of their general economic standing, black voters are disproportionately affected by mass immigration and trade deals like NAFTA. There is also an undercurrent of nationalism and tribalism that goes largely unreported. Many in the black community are unsettled by mass immigration from a cultural standpoint. A number of prominent black pastors and civil rights leaders, such as Charles Evers, brother of civil rights martyr Medgar Evers, have endorsed Trump because they believe he will be able to bring jobs to their communities. In less distinctly logical terms, Donald Trump is an icon in hip hop culture and has been for decades. Artists have written many songs mentioning him. His attitude and lifestyle is appreciated. Republicans have usually gotten single digit black support. There is no way he'll actually win the black vote, but if Trump can bump that number up to 15%, or in some way encourage a proportionately less amount of blacks to turn out to vote Democrat, he will have constructed a crucial piece in a winning coalition. There are signs that this may already be taking place, as despite Hillary Clinton's massive advantage over Bernie Sanders among black voters in the Democratic primaries, turnout among this demographic has dropped off dramatically compared to when Barack Obama was running. Turnout was down by 40% in Ohio, 38% in Florida, and 34% in North Carolina.[68]

Young Voters: Hillary Clinton's support among young voters is pitiful. She usually loses this group to Sanders by over 80%. Millennials are the generation perhaps most harmed by the race for globalization at any cost. They may not have lost jobs directly, but the economic climate has forced them to go to a university, with its accompanying tens or even hundreds of thousands of dollars of debt, just for a chance to make it. Many of them, upon graduating, cannot find work. Many also feel that they were scammed by Barack Obama, who promised them change but did not bring much of any. Trump's brand of 21st century American nationalism is also attractive to many young rightists who find themselves increasingly disaffected and alienated from the conservative movement. Very, very few young Americans identify as "conservative." Tellingly, there are indicators that Donald Trump has a large amount of grassroots support on college campuses,

STUMPED: HOW TRUMP TRIUMPHED

support which rivals that of Bernie Sanders. Meanwhile, Hillary Clinton and Ted Cruz seem to have none.[69] Certainly, Trump's being a symbol of rebellion against political correctness will likely have much to do with his attraction to the young, as many young people feel stifled by it, especially on those said college campuses. 2014's GamerGate saga was a sign of discontent amongst Millennials against the orthodoxy of social justice warriors – in fact; it was the first full-scale revolt against them in popular culture. Trump won't win this crowd, but like black voters, it is feasible that he could win enough of them and do better than Republicans have traditionally done and/or find a way to prevent enough from coming out to vote against him.

Union Workers: There have been rumblings that some major unions would endorse Trump. They certainly have been aversely affected by mass immigration and the trade deals of the past few decades. The forces of inertia and familiarity, as well as those entrenched in the leadership positions of these unions, will probably prevent any such endorsement. However, many of these workers could cross over to Trump's camp.

Lost Voters/Never Voted: This election has turned up many people that are so-called "lost voters." This group comprises those who haven't voted in many election cycles, even decades. It's also spurred those who haven't voted at all to come out for the first time. Most of the voters in these two categories that have come this season have turned out to vote for Donald Trump. I have a personal anecdote. My father fits the description of a "lost voter." He last voted in 1984 for Ronald Reagan. He has voiced his intention to come out and vote for Donald Trump.

Independents: Those stalwarts in the general popular revolt who feel alienated from both parties because of the actions of the optimates within them. Though registered independents often tend to lean toward one party or the other, and so the "swing voter" is a bit of a misnomer, thus far, Trump has done best in states with open or mixed primaries, where independents are allowed to vote for whatever candidate they choose. He's only lost one of these states, Wisconsin. Among this group, an anti-establishment, anti-globalization; pro-nationalist offer will probably do better than a status quo offer, especially given the pendulum effect on other issues such as political correctness.

These demographics can form a coalition to electoral victory, and it is these voters that form Donald Trump's strategy. He saw the market, made a strategic offer, and formulated his tactics and operations to leverage that offer to move this market of voters and achieve his strategic end. Trump's dominance in all geographic regions of the country except for those with relatively sparse population densities and his overwhelming victory in Florida, a state that is essentially made up of a cross-section of the entire American population, suggests what may be possible in a general election.[70]

Ultimately, the Trump movement, the realigning election of 2016, and the social atmosphere which led up to it, may just be the beginning of a new, seventh party political system in the history of the United States. From time to time, these systems shift as electorates realign, and the political ethos shifts with them. The beginning of one system and the end of another are associated with the realigning elections discussed earlier:

First party system: This evolved from the disputes between Alexander Hamilton and Thomas Jefferson, and in many respects, they are still with us today. Should the federal government be strong or weak vis a vis the states? What should be the balance between each? Should the Constitution be strictly or loosely interpreted? Would the country's economy be based on industry or agriculture? This system saw sparring between the Federalists, who got most of their support in New England, and the Democratic-Republicans, who got their support mainly in the South, while the mid-Atlantic would usually shift to the latter. It began in the Washington administration and ended in the Monroe administration, the Era of Good Feelings. The Jeffersonian Republicans won this battle, but would ultimately lose the war.

Second party system: This began in 1828, with the election of Andrew Jackson. In that election, the Democratic Party was created by Jackson and Martin van Buren. In turn, the Democrats were opposed to the Whig Party dominated by Henry Clay. Slavery became an increasingly important issue as the westward expansion of the country continued. Another big issue was finance, as the Whigs fought, ultimately unsuccessfully, to restore the Bank of the United States which had been ended by Andrew Jackson. As the country expanded westward and the power of the Abolitionist movement grew, tensions between the North, which had largely abolished slavery, and the South, which relied on it for its economy and had it ingrained deeply into its culture, also grew. The Whigs fell apart in the 1850's as the country descended further and further into turmoil. The Jeffersonian agricultural ethos still dominated this system politically in the form of the Democratic Party, but that dominance would soon come to a bloody end.

Third party system: The realigning election of 1860 which ushered Abraham

Lincoln into the White House brought this into being. The abolition of slavery, the first attempts at a civil rights revolution, and stricter control over the states through restraining devices like the 13th, 14th, and 15th Amendments as well as the Civil Rights Act of 1866, were ushered in by the Republican Party, which had arisen, and it dominated this era from its stronghold in the North. However, as Reconstruction ended and the federal government retreated, Southern Democrats chipped away at this first civil rights revolution, instituting Jim Crow laws. This was the beginning of the "Solid South," where the Deep Southern states would vote for Democrats in unbroken succession until 1964. This was also the era when the United States began to expand industrially and emerge as a world power. The Republican Party actively encouraged industrial growth. Though still not entirely complete, the Hamiltonian vision won, and has remained dominant ever since. Republicans also began to tackle civil service reform, an issue that had emerged as part of the Spoils System in the Jackson administration.

Fourth party system: Ushered in with the narrow, hard-fought victory of William McKinley in the realigning election of 1896, the beginnings of the parties as we know them today took place. McKinley, the Republican backed by big donors, brought forth the genesis of modern campaign finance, while his opponent, William Jennings Bryan, pioneered the art of modern campaigning by holding mass rallies all over the country, championing what we would call "the little guy." The major issues were the disparities of wealth that had taken place over the preceding decades of industrialization and the place America would hold in the world as it began to flex its muscle on the international stage. The Republicans dominated this system, but under Theodore Roosevelt and William Howard Taft, answered some earlier populist criticisms and instituted the Progressive Era, reforming business, banking, labor, financial, and other laws. In the latter phases of this era, immigration to the United States was virtually shut down and the Harding and Coolidge administrations were accused by some of engaging in policies which helped create a massive financial bubble. The system ended with the Great Depression and the election of 1932.

Fifth party system: Franklin Delano Roosevelt swept the Democrats into power amidst the misery of the Great Depression, and it was they who dominated. The era was marked by the greatest expansion of government in history in the New Deal and the parties become truly recognizable as Republicans first tried to stop it and then embraced it. The same was true of the latter stages of the era in Lyndon Johnson's Great Society programs. In addition to the emergence of the modern welfare state, the second civil rights revolution got underway late in this period with the support of many in both parties but with fierce opposition by Southern

Democrats. Internationally, the United States' role as global leader by its intervention and triumph in World War II was affirmed. This new international role was held to task by both Democratic and Republican administrations. The system ended in the election of 1968, when the New Deal Coalition fell apart.

Sixth party system: The present era, though we may indeed be seeing its last days. Perhaps it has even already ended. In the realigning election of 1968, the Solid South's collapse in 1964 was proven not to be a fluke. Richard Nixon's "Southern Strategy" rode a backlash against Democratic support, as seen in President Johnson, of the Civil Rights Movement. It paid off. Nixon put together a coalition of "law and order" conservatives that eventually evolved into the coalition dominant in Republican Party politics today. With the sole exception of Jimmy Carter's campaign in 1976, Republican dominance has been the status quo in the South ever since. Political power also shifted somewhat back to the South, as four of the seven presidents since Nixon (Carter, the Bushes, and Clinton) have been Southerners. Republicans returned to dominance of the presidency. Democrats began to find their way out of the wilderness under Bill Clinton and his New Left.

Seventh party system: This may have been ushered in beginning in 2008 with the election of Barack Obama and will possibly take its final form in 2016, especially should Trump win. The Democratic Party seems intent on going the social justice warrior route for now, if Hillary Clinton and Bernie Sanders' campaigns are any indication. Their globalism will continue for the time being under Hillary Clinton. Meanwhile, the 2016 election is a struggle to break away the Republican Party from both globalism and in some respects, the religious right, as many attacks on Donald Trump have come from that direction. The new Republican Party that emerges, especially if more candidates follow in Trump's wake, may indeed be that party of "common sense conservative," free market nationalism, marked by suspicion of big government and corporate welfare, and aligned toward an "Americans first" worldview. Eventually, the Bernie Sanders faction will likely wrest control of the Democratic Party and turn it away from globalism toward a "New New Deal," one concerned about economic fairness and civil rights issues, with an emphasis on the disproportionate racial outcomes of certain policies, all the while it purges the postmodernist social justice warriors. While the Republican Party in the seventh party system may be in some ways animated by the ghosts of Andrew Jackson and Theodore Roosevelt, the Democratic Party may be animated by those of Franklin Delano Roosevelt and William Jennings Bryan.

Perhaps this is too optimistic. Perhaps social justice warriors will completely take over the Democratic Party and that will be the focus of the realignment. Perhaps the Republican Party will realign in ways unforeseen. Maybe Trump is so unhinged that he forces the Republican Party to become a true Democrat-lite.

What is likely above all however, is that the election of 2016 has been and will continue to be a referendum on globalism, and given the success of Trump and Sanders, the public has resoundingly rejected it. The realigning election of 2016 will be a retrenchment in some ways from axiomatic, all-encompassing globalism, even if not done in precisely the ways envisioned here. The world is not the same as it was in the fifth and sixth party systems, and each system must respond to the demands of the time. This is the referendum of a realigning election.

The forces brewing in the Popular Revolt of 2016, and within the tents of each respective party, are bigger than Trump. This election may very well set the course of American politics for the next few decades, something Trump is likely keenly aware of.

12. Piecing it all Together

Now that Trump's foundation, tactics, operations, and strategy have all been laid out, it's helpful to sum up the model upon which predictions for 2016 can be made in his favor, premise by premise. In this way, it's possible to quickly reconstruct the political hurricane Trump has amassed around himself which almost all of the talking heads could not see.

First: Humans are usually not acting as rational, self-interested agents, but can be influenced by many, often completely irrational factors. Visceral cues are far more potent than rational ones.

Second: Humans are tribal animals that organize themselves in teams and in/out-groups. In such a structure, the strongest tribal leader, the one who inspires feelings in supporters that they'd want to follow him into battle, will usually have the most alluring leadership appeal. This is a factor closely related to masculinity. Thus, the candidate that can telegraph this strong, often masculine leadership ability will usually win.

Third: Problems arise that people seek answers to, and communications are the key to power. The candidate that dominates the most space on the issues people want solved and the communicational space upon which they are intermediated with will usually win.

Fourth: The candidate who has the strongest offense and the stronger frame to impose his will and deflect criticism will usually win.

Fifth: The more charismatic candidate, naturally or otherwise, will usually win.

Sixth: The candidate with the strongest social proof will usually win.

Seventh: The candidate with the strongest, better-known personal brand will usually win.

Eighth: The candidate with the strongest perceived offer to the most concerning issues of the time, the ones that people react to in the most visceral, rather than cerebral way, will usually win.

Ninth: The candidate benefitting from the pendulum effect, the reaction against the previous regime, will usually win.

To test these criteria, they can be scrutinized in the context of *all* previous presidential elections. Hindsight is, as they say, 20/20, and this model, like many, may be accused of adapting to fit these facts in hindsight in a general, unfalsifiable way. There is also the danger that some may level the charge that the criteria are subjective enough to fit the data in an ad-hoc fashion.

While I accept that these charges may be leveled, I stand by my theses. I believe that they take into account erratic human behavior in a way that is general enough to make a solid prediction of upcoming events, and that they are also specific enough to fit in with the information presented in the preceding chapters of this book and can be awarded accordingly. I believe they are about as good as can be given the glaring hole in all social sciences – that human beings cannot be reduced to behaving in laboratory conditions. In any event, we will see how predictive my criteria are soon enough.

2012: Barack Obama, seen as a charismatic, suave, smooth, cool guy who approved the operation to kill Osama bin Laden (establishing a masculine/war leader frame as the killer of a hated enemy of the American in-group) and who claimed to "save the American economy," beat Mitt Romney, who was regarded as a weak, vacillating, stiff in a suit who uttered lame phrases like "binders full of women," "the 47%," and seemed to have no offer to the electorate except saying what would get him elected. The continued abhorrence of the Bush administration guaranteed the lack of a pendulum favoring Romney. Furthermore, while Obama's personal brand had the accomplishments listed above; Romney's became tarred by the Obama campaign as a corporate raider at Bain Capital that cost workers their jobs, a frame that certainly was not alleviated by "the 47%" comment or Romney's overall demeanor. Obama's supporters were young and energized while Romney's seemed to be lame old farts, clearly establishing Obama as having superior social proof. Meanwhile, millions of normally Republican-leaning voters stayed home entirely.

2008: Barack Obama, the suave, young, charismatic man, beat John McCain, who was perceived as a crusty, grumpy old warmonger made worse by his not-quite-there running mate, Sarah Palin, whose self-deprecating personal brand quickly spoiled his own. The pendulum factor was very strongly on Obama's side, as the reaction against the Bush years was at its strongest point. People were clamoring for change, an offer Obama clearly made with his campaign slogans. Though McCain had a more impressive personal brand than Obama, Obama's social proof was far greater with his massive crowds of enthusiastic, energetic supporters. He also mounted the first effective social media campaign in history to dominate more communicational space than McCain could.

2004: George W. Bush, the lovable loser, who was still benefitting from his onsite presence at Ground Zero days after 9/11 (a very Thutmose-like moment), and his strong response in keeping the nation safe by commanding strikes in Afghanistan and Iraq, beat John Kerry, regarded by the public as the stiff in a suit trying to pose as a hunter while voting for and then against the war in Iraq. In this, the Bush campaign successfully slammed Kerry's personal brand as being that of an unprincipled flip-flopper, while Vietnam veterans late in the campaign came out against him with the "Swift Boat Veterans for Truth" ads, further torpedoing his strongest masculine factor as a Vietnam War hero who received three Purple Hearts. The pendulum was not quite in force, as, although Bush was hated by a large segment of the population, his offer on the very visceral issues of terrorism and national security was decisive. These were issues that Kerry could not convincingly dominate.

2000: An anomaly since George W. Bush lost the popular vote while winning the Electoral College. Neither candidate struck a particularly masculine tone, though Bush arguably had an advantage in the area compared to the stiffer Al Gore. The pendulum factor is tricky to define. Though many people wanted change, the Clinton years were a successful time for the country, so many others saw no need. George W. Bush did however have impressive social proof with his recent-president father. Al Gore probably had a more impressive personal brand, but the Bush brand was also already well-known, so Gore could not be said to have had a decisive advantage in the area. Bush was also probably more relatable to the general population than Al Gore and therefore more charismatic.

1996: Bill Clinton, the smooth, cool, suave guy beat Bob Dole, who was seen as lame and stodgy. Clinton's charisma was simply overwhelming in comparison to Dole's. In addition, the economy was booming, so there was no prominent pendulum factor. This further denigrated Dole's seemingly stale offers. Dole had an impressive personal brand as a World War II hero, but as the country's demographics shifted and Generation X continued to reach voting age, the war increasingly left prominence in the public memory. Dole couldn't compete with an impressive, charismatic, media savvy (and therefore spatially dominant) president who had the upper hand on the winning issues.

1992: Bill Clinton played the saxophone on Arsenio and cruised to victory over George H.W. Bush, often regarded as a wimp. Though Bush was a successful war leader in the Gulf War (although he did face some criticism for not removing Saddam Hussein) and therefore should have been reelected easily based on that masculine factor, he could not maintain frame on his failed tax promise. George H.W. Bush raised taxes when his big offer in 1988 was that he would not, which tarnished his personal brand. Further, a stinging recession was in play in the early 90's, and that, plus the 12-year-streak of Republicans in the White House since 1981, created a pendulum factor which favored Clinton. Arguably however, the spoiler presence of Ross Perot left this election as one in which the model can be said not to fully apply.

1988: George H.W. Bush, normally seen as a wimp (despite his World War II experience), beat the even wimpier poseur Michael Dukakis after a failed photo-op in an M1 Abrams tank. "Dukakis in the tank" has since become a trope for spectacular failures in the field of public relations. Bush's running mate, Dan Quayle, had numerous gaffes, including his bearing the brunt of "Senator, you're no Jack Kennedy" during the Vice Presidential debate that year in which he lost bigly on his frame, but these could not overcome the tank incident. Dukakis tried to look more masculine than George H.W. Bush and failed. This dominated the conversational space of the election. Further, the country was still doing well in the Reagan years, so there was not a big pendulum factor for change. Bush's offer of continuation was solid.

1984: Ronald Reagan, who had over the course of his presidency eschewed traditional relations with the Soviet Union and took on a far more challenging tone by proposing the Strategic Defense Initiative ("Star Wars") in 1983 to gut the nuclear threat of the Soviets, crushed Walter Mondale, the more passive candidate, in one of the biggest landslides in history. Reagan won every state except Mondale's native Minnesota. Reagan's answer to the attention on his advanced age was one of the most masterful displays of frame control in American political history: "I will not make age an issue of this campaign. I am not going to exploit, for political purposes, my opponent's youth and inexperience." Reagan was also known as the "great communicator" for a reason, and his "it's morning again in America" ad was one of the best political commercials in history, dominating the space of the media apparatus and implanting the idea that a renaissance was truly at hand. Reagan connected to the country with it. Certainly, no pendulum was present, despite relatively high unemployment (around 8%). Reagan's communicational abilities and massive charisma helped to prevent it.

1980: Ronald Reagan, who masterfully controlled frame in a masculine way with his "I am paying for this microphone" quip, first beat the comparatively wimpy George H.W. Bush in the Republican primary and then the hapless Jimmy Carter, who was widely seen as presiding over failures at home and abroad, most infamously in Iran, in the general election. Carter's "Malaise Speech" of 1979 may have been based on some logic, but a "crisis of confidence" is antithetical to masculinity and Reagan steamrolled to victory with his continuously strong frame, as also seen when he responded with "there you go again" to Carter in a debate. He also had optimistic offers and benefitted from the pendulum against the perceived failures of the Carter years, which included a recession and stagflation.

1976: Gerald Ford narrowly defeated Reagan in the Republican primary with the advantage of incumbency behind him, allowing him to best the more masculine candidate due to having the superior social proof. However, he ultimately lost to Jimmy Carter. Ford had a terrible personal brand due to his connection with and pardon of Richard Nixon and hence in the public mind, Watergate, which was a dominant theme. He also blundered badly in a debate, mentioning that there was "no Soviet domination of Eastern Europe," an almost intolerable deviation from facing down the Soviet enemy in the Cold War. This both impugned Ford's masculinity and displayed a bad offer on an existential issue. Carter's offer was as an honest outsider that would put Watergate behind the country, and he won in a close contest.

1972: Richard Nixon defeated George McGovern, who was lampooned as a near-pacifist, in one of the most total victories in history. McGovern's perceived leftist irresponsibility and inaction gave Nixon an easy oppositional brand to gut. McGovern certainly did not offer a masculine sense of strength. This plagued him throughout the entire campaign during a still-uncertain time with Vietnam and the Cold War. Nixon dominated all conversational space on this, and it displayed a bad offer on McGovern's part on an existential issue. Every state except McGovern's native Massachusetts went to the Nixon camp.

1968: A pivotal election in the country's history, as it was feeling confused and vulnerable amidst cultural change, racial tensions, and an unpopular war. In many respects, the atmosphere was similar to today, because it was a realigning election. In the midst of confusion in the Democratic Party after the assassination of Robert Kennedy, Richard Nixon staged one of the most epic political comebacks in American history, making huge offers to a confused country. He promised to restore order to the country while reassuring it that he had a plan for Vietnam. Nixon also displayed social proof lavishly, popularizing the term, "the silent majority" and campaigning with the provocative and actionable, buyer-oriented headline, "America needs Nixon now!" He dominated space by staging a number of very favorable interviews on television, acquiring a masculine frame as a strong, stoic leader to fill the vacuum in a confused country.[71] Further, Nixon had the pendulum squarely behind him as a reaction to the Johnson administration's Vietnam quagmire, and for more unsavory elements, the backlash against its civil rights agenda. Nixon narrowly defeated the sitting vice president, Hubert Humphrey, who put himself in a straitjacket over Vietnam (and therefore not dominating space on this huge, visceral issue). Humphrey was also far from the first choice of the party's grassroots and was tarnished in his personal brand in association with Johnson. Furthermore, Humphrey did not go for the jugular – he refused to reveal damning information that people connected to Nixon's campaign, specifically a friend of his by the name of Anna Chennault, were tampering with peace talks with the North Vietnamese. Thus, Humphrey failed to attack and dominate the space on yet another visceral issue,[72] even though Johnson's conveniently-timed bombing halt in North Vietnam was an equally dirty tactic.[73] Still, Nixon would likely have won by a larger margin were it not for George Wallace running an impressive third party campaign, which raises some questions as to whether any of Humphrey's mistakes would matter had the latter been absent, as Nixon probably would have won anyway.

1964: A fragile time in the nation, as the assassination of President Kennedy happened only months earlier. Former Vice President, now President, Lyndon Johnson defeated Arizona Senator Barry Goldwater in a huge landslide, taking every state but his opponent's own and a few Deep Southern states in rebellion against the Civil Rights Act of 1964. This was the only pendulum effect Goldwater benefitted from, but it was too minor. It was also the fracturing of the Solid South. No general pendulum effect was present to help Goldwater and Johnson labeled him a nutjob who was going to "use the bomb," dominating the conversational space around it and implanting a visceral, fearful idea into the minds of the electorate. In that regard, Johnson didn't need to even make much of an offer, just the sane one. Goldwater's personal brand was ruined, and his frame was not strong enough to reverse it. In fact, Goldwater's frame reinforced the public's fears of him with his numerous gaffes. To the electorate, he was associated with the death of "Daisy Girl."

1960: A very close election with huge turnout that may have been won by fraud in Illinois, so the model can be argued to not apply here, but several factors did benefit John F. Kennedy over Richard Nixon. First, 1960 was a recession year, which created the beginnings of a pendulum. Kennedy enhanced this pendulum factor by pushing the false idea that there was a "missile gap," wherein the Soviet Union had a lead on the United States in intercontinental ballistic missile technology – an existential fear of nuclear annihilation. Dominating that issue, Kennedy's masculine image also helped a great deal – he was young and good-looking in contrast to the elderly President Eisenhower (yet another pendulum effect). His very look displayed charisma because women found him handsome and men wanted to be like him – instant connection. He projected vigor while Nixon exhausted himself and had to go to the hospital for an extended stay,[74] even though it was Kennedy who was in fact the sicklier one with his Addison's disease that he hid from the public. Though Nixon enhanced his masculine reputation earlier in his career with his famous debate with the Soviet Premier Khrushchev over the merits of capitalism against Communism, this election, through the recency effect (see below), tarnished that reputation, because 1960 was also a pivotal year in the history of electioneering communications, as it hosted the first televised presidential debates. The first of these was the most famous. Nixon looked sloppy, unkempt, and nervous in contrast to the cool Kennedy – impugning his own masculinity while elevating Kennedy's. Additionally, Nixon's frame was off, as he often seemed to defer to Kennedy. While those who listened to the debate on the radio thought Nixon won, visual is far more powerful than mere audio, and television-watchers thought Kennedy won. The final humiliation came when President Eisenhower could not seem to remember anything of significance that his vice president had done, torpedoing Nixon's personal brand, social proof, and frame, and Kennedy was all too eager to dominate space with the quote.

1956: Largely a repeat of 1952, except Adlai Stevenson lost in an even bigger landslide. The lack of a pendulum hurt him even further. Whereas in 1952 there was one – *against* him as a Democrat, this year, there was not one *for* him. Talk about bad luck.

1952: As the nation found itself in the midst of the stalemated Korean War, fears of the Soviet Union abounded, and with a seemingly stagnant, corrupt Democratic machine in Washington, Dwight D. Eisenhower ran on the Republican line, benefitting from the pendulum effect. His opponent, Adlai Stevenson, could not come anywhere close to the immense prestige of Eisenhower's personal brand, which guaranteed a domination of all communicational space. Being a war hero, Eisenhower was automatically the more masculine, tribal leader candidate. Additionally, 1952 was the first election in which television played a major part, and Eisenhower dominated this medium with his social proof-displaying slogan, "I like Ike." The social proof was not merely one dimensional, as the ad displayed the political draft which led to his candidacy – the proof of the crowd, not the politicians, taking Ike to Washington. Stevenson was outflanked on all fronts.

1948: An election that was famously incorrectly called in several papers. President Truman was largely unpopular, and because of this pendulum effect, the Republican nominee, Thomas Dewey, seemingly believed he could just walk into the White House. His campaign appearances were relatively limited and this backfired in several dimensions. First, it ensured Dewey would not dominate conversational space. Second, it impugned his social proof because he could not build an audience by being so abstract. Third, it didn't allow him to build a convincing personal brand behind him. Fourth, it did not allow him to display any charisma. How could Dewey be charismatic or master crowd psychology if he was unseen, locked away in a tower on high? Truman in the meantime campaigned furiously across the country, getting himself out there, building his brand, connecting with his supporters.[75] All of these factors allowed Truman to pull off a stunning upset, despite the pendulum effect and the split in the Democratic vote that year. Connecting with the crowd matters!

1944: Franklin Delano Roosevelt ran against New York Governor Thomas Dewey, winning in a landslide. Roosevelt was at this point an effective war leader and revered elder statesmen. His social proof, charisma, masculinity, and personal brand were through the roof, and with the war going well in 1944, there was no pendulum effect for Dewey to take advantage of. To add insult to injury, FDR was able to maintain a strong frame when the Republicans attacked his dog Fala over the supposed expense to taxpayers that he had lavished on him. Instead, FDR spun it around to ridicule the Republicans, making them look like stiffs that were upset at a defenseless dog.[76] With all of this on Roosevelt's side, Dewey had no chance.

1940: A critical election held in a very confusing and ominous time. President Roosevelt, seeing the dangers of the beginnings of World War II and the lingering effects of the Great Depression, where unemployment was still over 20%, broke with the two-term tradition stretching back to George Washington and ran for a third term. Despite the sacredness of this Washingtonian legacy, in such uncertain times, the people opted to stay with the familiar – Roosevelt, who had an immense personal brand behind him as a respected, experienced, and comforting leader. Additionally, Roosevelt's Republican opponent, Wendell Willkie, dominated little space, as he largely agreed with many of FDR's policies both domestically and internationally. Therefore, Willkie could not make a better offer. His business background also left him open to being associated with the class of people that generated the Great Depression. Though Willkie forced Roosevelt to take an isolationist stance by pledging to "not send American boys to fight in any foreign war," it was not enough for him to win.[77]

1936: The nation was still in the midst of the Great Depression. Normally, this would favor Roosevelt's opponent, Alf Landon, by creating a pendulum effect. Yet, a slow, painful recovery was in place, even though several of Roosevelt's programs, notably the National Recovery Administration, were failures. However, other initiatives were successful and popular. Roosevelt was able to successfully make a compelling offer that he would continue to enact programs to alleviate the burdens of working Americans in the Depression and increase their morale, while Landon was basically nowhere to be seen. Landon had no personal brand, charisma, social proof, or compelling offer. He could not dominate any space on issues related to the depression. Additionally, Roosevelt was a masterful framer, taking the stance of "welcoming the hatred" of powerful financial interests that caused the economic crisis.[78] Roosevelt won all but two states. Landon could not even win his own home state of Kansas of which he was the sitting governor.

1932: The nation was in the worst depths of the Great Depression. The President, Herbert Hoover, essentially offered nothing, calling for voluntarism in business to alleviate its effects, making him look like a weak, un-masculine leader. In such an atmosphere, almost anyone could have won due to the massive pendulum, but Hoover made it worse when he cracked down on a gathering of World War I veterans which included some deaths, further denigrating his already-bruised personal brand associated with "Hoovervilles" (shantytowns popping up in public places). Franklin Delano Roosevelt swept to power in a massive landslide and realigned American politics.

1928: The roaring 20's continued with few signs of stopping, creating no pendulum effect for the Democratic candidate, Al Smith, to attach to and make an offer from. Herbert Hoover's personal brand, associated with the popular Calvin Coolidge, was at that point good. Al Smith's personal brand, on the other hand, was negative. As he was a Catholic, social conservatives used his religion against him, dominating space on a potential existential issue in his loyalty to the pope over the United States.[79] Smith was also associated with New York's Tammany Hall political machine, tarring further his personal brand. Hoover won in a rout. Smith could not carry his home state of New York.

1924: Despite the Teapot Dome scandal involving the recently-deceased Harding, Calvin Coolidge was popular because of the continued economic boom. Further, the Democratic Party, with John W. Davis at the helm, had a bad split, a reduction in the amount of space they could reasonably dominate at the worst possible time. With no effective counteroffers, Coolidge won easily.

1920: A strong reaction against World War I and its aftermath created a yearning for a return to normalcy, an offer that Warren Harding made to a weary electorate by campaigning against the Treaty of Versailles and American entrance into the League of Nations. International intervention was a very new thing in American history and many voters found it deeply unusual and unsettling, opting for Harding's offer, advertised by his slogan, "America first." While Harding's opponent, James M. Cox, had a vigorous campaign with Franklin Delano Roosevelt as his running mate, it was poorly organized,[80] and Harding's campaign mastered something of crowd psychology by getting his own voters to come to his front porch and hear him speak.[81] By controlling the voters' actions in this way, he got them to connect to him and invest in him, making it more likely they'd vote Harding. Additionally, the Harding campaign dominated communicational space with a blitz advertising campaign.[82] All of these factors led to a decisive victory.

1916: A very close election in a tense time, the major issue was obviously World War I. The famous slogan of the Wilson campaign was "he kept us out of war," signifying the incumbent president's offer to continue on that same course, reducing any pendulum effect. Wilson's opponent, Charles Evans Hughes, simply could not make a winning offer on other issues. Although the result was very close, Wilson had enough support to seal the deal on his spatial dominance of all the major issues.

1912: A very unique election, as there was an extremely strong third party candidate – former President Theodore Roosevelt, who had failed to secure the nomination of the Republican Party from the incumbent, William Howard Taft. Roosevelt chose to run on his Bull Moose Party line. With the Republican vote split (even though Taft won only a few states), the Democrat Woodrow Wilson won the election. Because of this split, the model can be argued to not have applied.

1908: Theodore Roosevelt, greatly disappointed that he had pledged not to run again, entrusted the job to his handpicked successor, William Howard Taft. Roosevelt was popular, and Taft thus had a good personal brand by his association with the incumbent president. The Taft campaign also undercut the personal brand of its opponent, William Jennings Bryan, by referring to his two losses in 1896 and 1900. Because of the progressive reforms of Theodore Roosevelt, Bryan was left with little room to maneuver to make a better offer. All the space was dominated. Additionally, because Roosevelt was popular, there was no pendulum for Bryan to take advantage of.

1904: Theodore Roosevelt sought a term in his own right, competing against Alton B. Parker. Both candidates made similar offers to the electorate, such as the gold standard and action on antitrust issues (even though Parker tried to differentiate himself),[83] but Roosevelt's masculinity factor, his vigor and energy, his personal brand as the incumbent in office that was a former war hero, and his charisma, were simply too much. He won a solid victory.

1900: A rematch of 1896. This time, however, William McKinley had both the advantage of incumbency as well as victory in the Spanish-American War behind him, giving him recent masculine, tribal war leadership credibility. The booming economy at the time helped to ensure that there would be no pendulum effect that Bryan could take advantage of.[84] New York Governor Theodore Roosevelt as his running mate gave McKinley ample social proof due to his association with the famed commander of the Rough Riders. Roosevelt's whirlwind, charismatic speaking tour added to the effect. Furthermore, Bryan tarred his own brand by criticizing the hard-won gains of the Spanish-American War.[85] The result was a decisive victory for the McKinley campaign.

1896: One of the most pivotal elections in American history. Money entered politics as never before, opening new avenues of communication and buying new levels of influence. The country was in a bad depression stemming from the Panic of 1893, which would normally favor the challenging party, the Republicans, in William McKinley. Yet, William Jennings Bryan strongly repudiated Grover Cleveland's economic policies in favor of Free Silver[86] to bring inflation and looser money to the economy, realigning the Democratic Party and helping to take advantage of the pendulum effect. Bryan invented modern campaigning by going all over the country to hold rallies, building up enthusiastic crowds and bringing a large amount of social proof to his campaign,[87] while William McKinley used the strategy of getting voters to come to his locale to hear him speak – getting them all invested in him.[88] Bryan was a charismatic man, spellbinding his crowds all over the country, but William McKinley outspent him by a great amount, dominating advertising and communicational space. Additionally, though the depression was still ongoing, the nation had seen the worst of the panic, so Bryan's offer of Free Silver was not as potent as it may have been had the election been held a year or two earlier. He was thus losing the pendulum effect's maximum. Ultimately, McKinley won in a close contest with extremely high turnout.

1892: The Democrat Grover Cleveland staged one of the biggest political comebacks of all time and became the only president to serve two non-consecutive terms. Cleveland offered a gold standard to the electorate, while the incumbent Benjamin Harrison favored gold and silver backing of money. Cleveland also pledged to reduce the McKinley tariff, which was unpopular with a great deal of voters, swinging the pendulum in his direction.[89] Neither campaign was vigorous, but Cleveland was a well-known brand and did spend more money to dominate communicational space, which paid off.[90] There was also a vigorous third party, populist run under James B. Weaver, which carried a few states and began to set the tone for the Progressive Era to come.

1888: This election was another anomaly, as the incumbent Grover Cleveland won the popular vote but lost the Electoral College, so the model arguably does not fully apply. Benjamin Harrison (grandson of William Henry Harrison) suffered a scandal during the "Blocks of Five" affair in which the Republicans were accused of directly buying votes, but the Republican official who had concocted the scheme, W.W. Dudley, held his frame.[91] Cleveland, however, did not mount a vigorous campaign. He did not reach out to voters – so how could he connect to them, master their psychology, and be charismatic? Harrison did bring voters to him to dominate communicational space, and by default, was more charismatic than the absent Cleveland.[92]

1884: In a close election, Grover Cleveland took the White House for the Democrats for the first time since 1856. Both candidates had problems with their personal brands, as the Republican, James G. Blaine, was known to be caught in influence peddling.[93] This would normally benefit Cleveland, known as "Grover the Good," due to his fight against the Democratic Party machine in New York's Tammany Hall. The Blaine campaign, however, attacked Cleveland for fathering an illegitimate child. Cleveland demonstrated masterful frame and admitted that the child might have been his. As such, he said, he had made sure that he and his mother received the proper care. This reinforced his frame and brand of honesty, in contrast to Blaine's corruption.[94] In contrast, Blaine was caught up in his own sex scandal, and he could not maintain a strong frame against the accusers.[95] Finally, the Cleveland campaign took advantage of a massive anti-Catholic gaffe emanating out of the Blaine campaign, dominated the space on it, and fractured his support.

1880: The Democratic candidate, Civil War hero Winfield Scott Hancock, attacked his rival, James A. Garfield, over involvement in a scandal involving the transcontinental railroad, but the charges never really stuck. With memories of the Civil War still fresh, meanwhile, the Republicans used that road, known as "waving the bloody shirt," an existential issue, with continued success. Though Hancock was probably the more masculine candidate, the Democratic Party's association with the Civil War was still very bad for its brand. The Garfield campaign also hammered the Democrats on their stance about the tariffs that helped factory workers in the north, portraying them as unsympathetic to American labor, while the Hancock campaign blundered and could not hold frame on the issue, appearing inconsistent. Garfield was in trouble when the Morey Letter, which appeared to be from him and favoring Chinese immigration, came out, but it was later shown to be forged, which kept his frame solid. [96] In the end, Hancock's lack of dominance on the tariff issue and his failure to puncture Garfield's personal brand cost him this extremely close, razor-thin election.

1876: An anomalous election in which the winner, Republican Rutherford Birchard Hayes, won the Electoral College by a single vote but lost the popular vote to Democrat Samuel Tilden. A very strong pendulum favored Tilden, as he was running amidst the backlash of the significant corruption of the Grant administration as well as nearly two decades of unbroken Republican rule. Tilden's personal brand was particularly suited to riding the pendulum concerning corruption, as he had made a name for himself fighting it in the party machine of Tammany Hall and its kingpin, William "Boss" Tweed.[97] The Republicans ran on the usual questions of national loyalty stemming from the Civil War, but they did not hit nearly as hard due to the pendulum shift. Yet, the Democratic strategy also had a dark undercurrent, as it relied on suppression of the black vote in the South. The ballots in several states adding up to 20 electoral votes had problems as allegations of fraud dogged them. These votes would prove decisive, and in one of the most complex deal making processes in American history, Hayes was awarded the votes in exchange for the end of Reconstruction.[98]

1872: The personal brand of Ulysses S. Grant, triumphant victor of the Civil War, was unassailable, even when faced with questions of corruption. The ad-hoc party opposed to him, the Liberal Republicans, wanted to end Reconstruction, and their candidate, Horace Greeley, didn't even live to the end of the election that year.

1868: The pendulum swung rapidly against the sitting president, Andrew Johnson, who had taken power after Lincoln's assassination. The Radical Republicans, who wanted far stricter Reconstruction demands on the defeated South, were in the ascendant. With a still-devastated South, there was no prospect of a real challenge to the Republicans, and nominating Grant, with his immensely prestigious personal brand as the victor of the Civil War, sealed the deal.

1864: A critical election, as the Civil War was still raging. The cost of the war during the interceding years to the states still in the Union had been very high, and there was a considerable anti-war movement in the Copperheads in the remaining Union states. Abraham Lincoln was certainly not as revered in his own time as he is now. What was his personal brand? He was a man who was associated with a bloody, brutal war. A series of setbacks early in 1864 hurt his cause and campaign against his former subordinate, General George McClellan. Yet, the Democrats were splintered between the Copperheads and pro-war Unionists from the start. All the while, Lincoln's brand recovered with General William T. Sherman's victories in the Deep South that year, including his infamous "March to the Sea." This, combined with the withdrawal of General John C. Fremont from the race[99] doomed the Democrats and Lincoln won in a landslide.

1860: A confused nominating process in the Republican Party eventually brought Lincoln the nomination. This realigning election, where the Republican Party, based in the North, would dominate and usher in the third party system, was pivotal. It highlighted the coming fracturing of the Union and the deep regional divide that was quickly reaching critical mass. There was only one issue in this election – the future of the Union, and sectional loyalties carried the greatest weight. These sectional loyalties ultimately splintered the Democratic Party into northern and southern factions. Abraham Lincoln was a dark horse prior to getting the Republican nomination, but he cleverly dominated space by buying niche newspapers that catered to key demographics, spellbound his audience with his charisma at Cooper Union in New York, and released a book of his famous debates with Stephen A. Douglas, who was also running for president that year.[100] Additionally, his operatives at the convention stuffed the crowd with fake delegates who got in on counterfeit tickets they had printed. The fake delegates chanted Lincoln's name, giving him instant social proof.[101] This helped him to stage a come-from-behind victory over multiple ballots. As the contest was split four ways between Lincoln on the Republican line, his old Illinois rival Stephen A. Douglas on the Democratic line, the sitting Vice President John C. Breckinridge on the Southern Democratic line, and John Bell on the Constitutional Union line, and given that a large enough plurality of the North had by this point come to thoroughly detest slavery, it was from that point mostly a question of math, a Nate Silver, rather than a *Stumped* election. Abraham Lincoln was viewed by the South as irreconcilable to its interests over the slavery issue. Nevertheless, because Lincoln's northern base had by far the most electoral votes; and the pro-Union vote was split between Douglas and Bell in the South,[102] he won the divided, four-way contest.

1856: Sectional tensions began to boil over as the future of slavery and the new territories started to fracture the nation at the seams. As the Whig Party disintegrated over the preceding years, the Republican Party, staunchly anti-slavery, formed in its vacuum. John C. Fremont was the Republican nominee. Opposing him was the Democrat James Buchanan and former President Millard Fillmore, who was making a run on the American Party line. While the Republicans campaigned vigorously against slavery, the Democrats supported popular sovereignty (wherein the population of a new territory could vote as to whether to allow slavery in the future state or not) and played to the existential issue of the Republicans' ability to fracture the Union if they won. Furthermore, Fremont's personal brand was blemished by the American Party's spreading rumors that he was a Catholic, which he was unable to repudiate.[103] That frame prevailed in favor of the Democrats, as did their offer of assuring that the Union would remain together.

1852: The Democratic candidate, Franklin Pierce, ran against the Whigs under Mexican-American War hero, General Winfield Scott. Yet, Pierce was also a war hero, serving as a brigadier general in the conflict, which cancelled out a masculinity/tribal leader advantage for either candidate. With the Whigs fractured and confused over the slavery issue, the Democrats had a relatively easy path to victory, borne out in the results.

1848: With the successful conclusion of the Mexican-American War, the Whigs dominated the existential issue of the future of slavery in the new territories and what it would mean for the Union. The personal brand and masculinity factors of the Whig candidate, General Zachary Taylor, Mexican War hero, essentially won the election by themselves, as his opponents, the Democrat Lewis Cass and the Free Soiler former President Martin van Buren could not compete.

1844: The Democratic Party nominated James Knox Polk to oppose the seasoned campaigner, the Whig Henry Clay. The principal issue of the campaign was the annexation of Texas, an existential one which would affect the balance of power between the North and South. Incumbent President John Tyler wanted Texas annexed as a slave state. Clay cautioned that this would be disastrous for the fragile status quo between the sections of the Union. Yet, this cautious diplomacy was no match for the far more energetic platform of Manifest Destiny by the ardent expansionist Polk, which connected far more viscerally to the American character. Polk, ever the consummate Jacksonian, was therefore perceived as both more masculine and more charismatic than his opponent. Clay had a more well-known personal brand than Polk, but could not compete with his energetic message and stupendous offer of new territories. Clay's frame on the slavery issue was also severely shattered in this election, splintering his natural base.[104]

1840: With the country mired in a deep depression due to Andrew Jackson's bank wars, almost anyone could have won. The pendulum effect was overwhelming against the incumbent, Democrat Martin van Buren. Yet the Whigs seemingly didn't get the memo. Instead of nominating their strongest figure, Henry Clay, they nominated William Henry Harrison, a general who won the Battle of Tippecanoe (really more like a slaughter of outgunned people) because the Whigs thought that he would be the candidate to most closely resemble Andrew Jackson.[105] This campaign was also the first to bear a notable slogan – "Tippecanoe and Tyler too." It isn't exactly a great one that deeply connects to the crowd or displays social proof, but it did promote Harrison's personal brand as a masculine war hero. Harrison also held a strong frame. When the Democrats accused him of being an old man who sat in a log cabin drinking hard cider, the Harrison campaign took the label and adapted it, using it for songs and imagery, displaying immense social proof and connection with the public. Martin van Buren, on the other hand, was portrayed as an out of touch elite. The fact that this was not true – that van Buren came from a modest background and Harrison from one of affluence, was entirely immaterial.[106] What mattered was that *it seemed true at the time*. In the end, Harrison's offer to staunch the depression, an offer that came from a, to the public, authentic character, was not going to be passed up.

1836: This was a unique election, as the Whigs ran four candidates, including the future President Harrison, in different regions to splinter the electoral vote and put the election to the House of Representatives. The plan failed however, because van Buren was a consummate organizer who dominated space throughout the election and got his supporters to the polls.[107] Further, his association with Andrew Jackson was good for his personal brand. He won comfortably.

1832: With the immensely popular Andrew Jackson running for reelection, almost nothing would be able to stop him. The pendulum was squarely on his side in addition to all his other assets. Jackson's opponent, Henry Clay, attempted to outmaneuver him and dominate space on the defining issue of the election – the fate of the Second Bank of the United States, but he held a rock-solid frame, vetoing the renewal bill and declaring that by doing so, he was championing the interests of the common people against a plutocratic class, sticking with his brand and platform. He won in a landslide.

1828: A pivotal, realigning election that ushered in the second party system. It was also without question the nastiest, most vicious campaign in history.[108] After the "corrupt bargain" of 1824, Jackson moved with a significant pendulum behind him, as the incumbent John Quincy Adams had been a hamstrung president throughout his entire term by Jackson's partisans in congress. The election was not about issues, but character – personal brands. The Adams campaign mounted vigorous (and true) attacks against Jackson. None of them stuck. Meanwhile, Jackson tarred Adams with the most scandalous (and false) headlines, such as his procuring a young American virgin for the Czar of Russia during his diplomatic career.[109] Once more, hyperbole or outright lies dominated more space than truth, proving that the biggest ones are often the best.[110] Meanwhile, in contrast to the highly masculine tribal war leader in Jackson, Adams tarnished his own masculinity by making a fool of himself in the groundbreaking ceremony on the Chesapeake and Ohio Canal. While digging the first hole, he hit a root and then kept hitting it. This labeled him as an out of touch elite who couldn't even work a shovel. The image was made even worse when the Adams campaign tried to display Jackson's lack of intelligence by advertising the misspellings of words in letters he had written. The electorate itself promptly took that as an insult on *themselves* from a still further out of touch elite.[111] Controversy existed over the opinion of the deceased Thomas Jefferson, with the Adams faction attempting to prove Jefferson detested Jackson. In this, they produced some first-hand accounts from witnesses. Yet, the Jackson faction held its own frame, and they seemed to produce the best evidence in the form of an unreleased letter from Jefferson declaring his alarm at the expanding federal government and the elite institutions surrounding it, such as the banks – key issues of Jackson's.[112] Jackson's frame also held strong when the Adams faction called him a "jackass" – an image that he promptly took as the mascot of his own Democratic Party.[113] In the end, Jackson's masculinity, charisma, personal brand, and his domination of the minds of the public were overwhelming and he won in a walk.

1824: This election was the first in which the popular vote had a real influence.[114] There were numerous candidates. The heir apparent to James Monroe was John Quincy Adams, but he was opposed by William Crawford and Henry Clay, two career politicians like himself. Also in the mix was Andrew Jackson, the immensely popular victor of the Battle of New Orleans in 1815 and conqueror of Florida. With this personal prestige and popularity behind him as a vigorous, masculine conqueror, Andrew Jackson won both the popular vote and, critically, the Electoral College. Yet, in an anomaly that produced one of the biggest scandals in American electoral history, Andrew Jackson did not win the required number of electoral votes to carry the election. With the splintered electoral vote, the ballot went to the House of Representatives, where Henry Clay was the speaker. In this ballot, the House voted for John Quincy Adams as president, who then promptly appointed Clay his secretary of state (the heir apparent position in those days). This scandal became known as the "corrupt bargain," and it dominated the conversational space for the next four years.

1820: The incumbent James Monroe was running for reelection unopposed. The Era of Good Feelings was in full swing.

1816: James Monroe of the Democratic-Republican Party, founding father, former secretary of state, wounded in action fighting alongside Washington at Trenton, ran against Rufus King on the Federalist line. By this point, the Federalist Party was floundering after having been shut out of power for so long. It would in fact be its last campaign. With the War of 1812 having ended on very favorable terms for a country which had been so badly defeated, the timing of the pendulum was off for King and the Federalists, and they could not take advantage of it. Additionally, the Hartford Convention a couple of years prior, in which there was talk of secession amongst New England Federalists, tarnished their, and by extension, King's brand.[115] The Federalists also could not dominate much space on various other issues, as compromises in the Madison administration gave Federalists much of what they wanted, such as a new national bank and tariffs.[116] This left them with no real offer to make. Additionally, Monroe had a great personal brand and social proof because of his connection to Presidents Jefferson and Madison. He could rightly advertise himself as the heir apparent, one who would be futile to oppose.

1812: The incumbent James Madison ran for reelection on the Democratic-Republican line and was opposed by DeWitt Clinton on the Federalist line. Madison's immense social proof and brand were factors in his favor, and the war declaration created a call to go with the familiar – Madison. As much of the fighting and certainly the worst of the war had not happened yet, this failed to create a pendulum that the Federalists could take advantage of. Clinton couldn't make a compelling counteroffer to Madison's social proof and stable leadership, refusing to dominate space as an anti-war candidate.[117]

1808: President Jefferson's second term was very disastrous for him and for New England in particular, which was chaffing at the Embargo Act of 1807 which made foreign trade illegal. This would typically create a pendulum against Jefferson and the Democratic-Republicans, but the country at this time was not quite what Alexander Hamilton had envisioned it to be (a financial, manufacturing, and industrial power), and in the agricultural ethos of the day, an economic system which prevailed in the rest of the country, the Embargo Act was simply not an existential issue which the Federalists, with Charles C. Pinckney at the helm, could make a strong offer on. Furthermore, James Madison's social proof – his association with Jefferson going back so many years, was immense. He was also Jefferson's secretary of state. By this time, the secretary of state was considered the heir apparent, the next in line to be president. Madison was the first to really benefit from this expectation. It certainly implanted the idea that people were supposed to vote for him. Madison's personal brand tied directly to this social proof on multiple fronts.

1804: The immensely popular Thomas Jefferson won reelection in a landslide against the Federalist Charles C. Pinckney, who only carried two states. There was simply no pendulum for Pinckney to take advantage of or an offer for him to make to the electorate.

1800: A realigning election which was one of the nastiest in history. With the French Revolutionary Wars in full swing in Europe, Thomas Jefferson and his Democratic-Republican Party viciously attacked the incumbent John Adams and the Federalists over their seemingly overtly pro-British foreign policy and the Alien and Sedition Acts, which they claimed were antithetical to constitutional government and threatening of American liberty. This was an existential issue that Jefferson dominated a huge amount of space on. What could be worse than a coming tyranny? The fears of the French Revolution stoked by the Federalists simply could not compete with the Democratic-Republican message on these Acts, especially as seen in the Virginia and Kentucky Resolutions authored in secret by Jefferson and Madison, which threatened nullification by the states of unconstitutional federal laws. While neither Jefferson nor Adams were particularly masculine tribal leaders, Jefferson was seen by a great many in the country as the defender of liberty against an encroaching and increasingly intrusive federal government, a suspicion that was (and is) still very much alive, emanating back to the days debating ratification of the Constitution itself. Additionally, John Adams was seen by many Federalists, including Alexander Hamilton, as not going far enough, and he faced a serious challenge in the campaign from within his own party. Another problem for Adams was that his 1796 victory was so narrow that his opponents labeled him as "a president of three votes,"[118] further tarring his personal brand as well as his social proof. While Jefferson might be a "Jacobin,"[119] this relatively abstract thought was probably less influential than the visible lack of social proof and accused aristocratic tyranny of Adams and the Federalists. The Democratic-Republicans also dominated far more space, as the Federalists did not actively campaign amongst the people.[120] In one of the most complex conclusions in history, Jefferson won the Electoral College, but because both he and his running mate Aaron Burr technically received the same amount of electoral votes, he did not win the presidency immediately, and the election went to the House of Representatives. After many tries, Jefferson narrowly won the vote in the House after Alexander Hamilton threw his support behind him over Burr. Because of this complexity, and because Jefferson ultimately won the election due to the Three-Fifths Compromise in the Constitution, wherein slaves were counted as three-fifths of a person in the census,[121] the model arguably doesn't apply, despite Jefferson following it well.

1796: With the revered George Washington retiring from office, the ugliness of presidential politics began. A bitterly divided contest between John Adams, Washington's vice president, and Thomas Jefferson, the former secretary of state, commenced, with the Federalist Party supporting Adams and the Democratic-Republicans supporting Jefferson. The dominant issue was foreign policy and the chaos engulfing Europe as a result of the French Revolution. Yet, Jefferson and the Republicans were thrown off frame by the public backing of the French Ambassador prior to the election,[122] making the warnings of the Federalists about the chaos in Europe too great to ignore.

1792: No one opposed George Washington's reelection and he again secured all electoral votes.

1788-1789: With his immense prestige and personal brand, his unquestionable masculinity as a successful and motivating war leader, with the reverence of a public that viewed him as a father figure, and with the domination of space in the minds of all in the country, no one questioned that George Washington should be the first President of the United States. He also benefitted from the pendulum against the chaotic years of the Articles of Confederation and the hope of alleviation that ratifying the Constitution would bring.

Now that this vast history has been briefly discussed, it is imperative to try to project for the 2016 election:

Donald Trump vs. Hillary Clinton:

Donald Trump and Hillary Clinton each have well-known personal brands. Everyone knows them, so the familiarity factor will be present for both sides. Both have high unfavorable ratings, but Donald Trump is far more colorful and dominating of the media communicational space. Using his mastery of the media – both traditional and new, Trump is far more adept at crafting his own message and brand, where Hillary's penchant for isolation – the carefully constructed appearances and staged photo ops – leave her more vulnerable to having others define her brand and message for her. Additionally, given the Popular Revolt of 2016, where insiders are out and outsiders are in, Hillary's brand will already be tarnished by default. Making her brand even worse is her unpopular and scandalous history. As a result, people do not trust her. She will not be able to make a compelling offer to an electorate in revolt, where Donald Trump can and has. If the upset results of the Democratic Michigan primary are any consideration, Hillary Clinton's stances, particularly on trade with her close association with deals like NAFTA and the TPP, will be extremely unpopular. This will be especially so in the Rust Belt. This is in contrast to Trump, who is making an alternative offer. Hillary Clinton will undoubtedly try to throw a counteroffer into the mix, as she has recently attempted to say she's been "tough with China on trade," but few who haven't already made up their minds to vote for her are likely to believe her. Additionally, with Donald Trump's frame being what it is, he will take any attack against him, spin it into a positive, and throw it back at Hillary Clinton, or simply ignore the attack and counterattack with a much stronger stance – as seen with her attempts to brand Trump as a sexist in January. There, Trump responded with an Instagram video associating her with her husband's sordid history, as well as with Bill Cosby. Hillary Clinton's history on foreign intervention, where she voted for the invasion of Iraq, will also be unpopular in a general election. She is disliked by many white Democrats, who have complained about her perceived pandering to minorities while ignoring their own concerns. These crossover voters will give Trump strong demographics, while it's unlikely that the Obama coalition will turn out in as great numbers to vote for Hillary Clinton, who cannot connect with her own audience and lacks the charisma to energize her base. Great deals of people find her very voice repulsive. Given her negative social proof, where she is endorsed by many that people see as corrupt, but cannot convincingly mobilize the voters at large, the electorate in revolt will favor Trump. Additionally, should a terrorist attack occur on American or European soil, Trump's domination of the space on the issue will favor him, perhaps bringing people to vote for him that didn't want to previously, because his plan seems to be the only game in town on this very visceral threat. The electorate also has such distaste for Hillary Clinton that a great deal of people will not vote for her under any circumstances, even if afraid of Trump.

Many however, won't vote for either of them. This leaves the possibility of third party spoilers to disrupt the model, or one of very low turnout that throws the election off in some way and truly makes it unpredictable by any model. This prediction, of course, assumes that the latter won't happen and that the former will remain too small to matter, as it has in most American elections.

Donald Trump vs. Bernie Sanders:

This election, though unlikely, will be far more difficult for Trump to win, even if he should pivot and soften his rough edges to make people less afraid of him. Though polls should always be taken with caution, especially as early in the process as the election cycle currently is, no poll has yet shown Trump ahead of Sanders in a general election scenario.

Sanders can, quite simply, appeal to an electorate in revolt, where Hillary Clinton cannot. Just as Trump has done, Sanders is making offers on existential issues similar to Trump, like trade and foreign intervention. Sanders has ample social proof with his young, enthusiastic, energetic supporters, and his slogans work the crowd, call to action, and enhance his social proof, making his offer more appealing. Sanders does not dominate space to the extent that Trump does and his frame is far weaker, which would give him difficulties in puncturing holes in Trump's personal brand, but given the highly unfavorable opinion many already have of Trump, Sanders wouldn't need to do as much of this kind of attacking. Yet, it is doubtful that any attacks would stick, and equally so that Sanders would be able to fend off Trump's artillery were it to come at him. Trump's crossover appeal would be less in this general election, but Sanders' inability to connect with a key base of the Democratic coalition in minority voters, as seen in the Democratic primaries thus far, would be a problem, particularly if Trump does the soft, general election pivot that seems likely and his popularity with the black vote is, as is quite possible, underreported. Trump's victory in Florida may also suggest an underreporting of his popularity with Hispanics (a nebulous demographic that is far from as monolithic as the talking heads often seem to believe).[123] Furthermore, Sanders has a lack of the dominance and masculinity that Trump has. Sanders was infamously bullied away from his own microphone by hooligans at one of his rallies in the summer of 2015. In a world of uncertainty, Trump will project a kind of strength that Sanders wouldn't be able to, and should a terrorist attack occur on American or European soil prior to the election, which is sadly not unlikely, it would only strengthen that frame even more. (Unfortunately, it only took a week after originally composing these passages about terrorist attacks for one to take place – the bombings in Brussels on March 22nd. I suspect that even more will occur prior to the election.) This is the space Trump attempted to dominate with his "Muslim ban." Trump is also the kind of person that you instinctively believe could lead you into battle. Sanders is not, and that lack of masculinity and tribal leadership will especially hurt him in the case of more terrorist attacks. Finally, while Sanders' "socialist" brand won't hurt him significantly in 2016 (the word just isn't the boogeyman it once was, especially to Millennials who grew up after the end of the Cold War), the majority of Americans are upset about current immigration levels – an issue offer that Sanders cannot make, but Trump can. Over time, as events unfold and Trump goes on the attack against Sanders, Trump could well pull out a victory with his superior frame, charisma, masculinity factor, and offer on immigration. As long as he can pivot enough to not motivate huge numbers to come out against him, he should prevail.

Assumptions:

These projections of course assume a few things – firstly, that Trump has no massive gaffe. This will likely not be the case, based on the way Trump has run his campaign thus far, deflecting all criticism. The second assumption is that Trump will find a way to alleviate the fear that many feel of him. Trump's biggest weakness, to quote Scott Adams, is that "he scares half the country."[124] This is absolutely true, and there are some signs that some of the crossover votes in the primaries from independents and Democrats on the Republican ballot have been from those who are scared of him and are voting against him. Though this is likely a relatively small problem, as those open and mixed primaries are where he has tended to do best, it could pose a significant threat in the general election. If Trump doesn't find a way to pivot and calm the fears of those afraid of him, he will absolutely have a tougher time winning the general election and may well lose it, and lose it big, despite his great sales skills and the ongoing popular revolt.

Yet, it is likely that Trump will indeed pivot when he wins the nomination or even before. What we've seen of him so far are classic overshoot tactics as he explains in his *The Art of the Deal*. The ongoing popular revolt ensures that there is a great deal of anger out there, and Donald Trump can also turn that fear into anger – anger at Washington, especially if he should find himself up against Hillary Clinton, as seems almost certain. Anger will also be directed at the globalist optimate class that she so perfectly personifies. Additionally, there are two final phenomena of unconscious, illogical human decision-making of import to this campaign that have thus far gone undiscussed. These are what are known as the primacy and recency effects.

Human beings tend to prioritize later information over earlier information. This is what is known as the recency effect. If asked to remember information on a list, about a product or a person, etc., we have an unconscious bias favoring the most recent information. If you research an issue, for instance, you'll tend to be unconsciously drawn to the information you heard most recently about it.

Conversely, there is the primacy effect, where humans are known to prioritize the first bits of information on the list, about the product, etc. that they are looking at. This is partly why first impressions matter so much. Those first impressions will be remembered and ultimately acted upon over later impressions.

One thing that I think illustrates these two concepts is word puzzles. Try to figure this jumbled word out:

Tweor.

How long did it take you? Did you think of a certain word associated with Donald Trump?

These word puzzles are made immensely easier if the first and last letters of the jumbled word are left intact. In many respects, we recognize words solely because of their first and last letters. This is probably a very practical (and brief, for the purposes of this book) show of the recency and primacy effects in action.

In other words, the recency and primacy effects guarantee that the vast majority of information in a presidential campaign lies mostly dormant. This is especially so in a 24/7, never-ending news cycle. We only have limited attention spans, particularly in comparison to the vast universe of information out there, and this forces us to prioritize. The primacy and recency effects are that prioritization in action.

Because of the recency effect, Donald Trump can easily take on a softer tone in the general election and have that be given priority. Have you noticed that most of the outrages in the media about Trump generally wane and are in turn replaced by new outrages? Around the time I began writing this book, his "failure to disavow David Duke and the KKK" was the huge outrage of the moment. As I'm finishing it, it's not even mentioned anymore.

Timing is everything in politics in part because of the recency effect. Information that comes out favoring the stances of one candidate over the other nearest to the election has immense value. This is why a terrorist attack on American or European soil close to Election Day would favor Trump in a big way.

On the other hand, Trump will always be dogged by accusations of racism and bigotry because of the primacy effect, since he began his campaign with his infamous "Mexicans are rapists" comment. That, to him, was probably the cost of supreme dominance of the space on the existential issue of immigration, but if he can be criticized over one thing regarding his sales skills, this would be it. He could have dominated space on immigration strongly to begin with in his announcement speech, and then have done the outrage about a month later if he needed to establish more authority and drag the Overton Window further, in order to avoid a negative primacy effect.

In a general election, Trump, through all of his methods discussed earlier, can pivot to neutralize the fear with the recency effect, and act in other ways to counter the primacy effect amongst certain people. Picking a woman or minority running mate would be one such way. Ben Carson's endorsement of Trump matters a lot in that regard.

There is also the danger of Trump being a niche brand that benefits from repetitive advertising amongst some, but not most of the market.[125] In this scenario, Trump would be a popular commodity amongst a plurality of the GOP base and some working class independents that lean Republican anyway, but not with a broad enough swathe of the electorate to win the White House. Amongst the rest, his repetitive advertising won't work, because other voters don't and never will fall into Trump's niche. This is not an insignificant danger, and if this turns out to be true, it will lead to his loss on Election Day. The niche brand scenario, along with the fear factor, are the biggest dangers to the Trump campaign, and worse, the niche brand will be very hard indeed, if not impossible, to overcome. Yet, the success of Trump in open primaries, the number of Democrats switching parties to Republican, his general plurality of support in the primaries amongst all demographics, and the hugely increased Republican turnout, suggest that the niche brand scenario may not be the most likely one, and that Trump has a widespread, elastic base.

Both of these projections also assume that the Republican Party holds together and does not form a separate "independent conservative" campaign or anything like it. If the Party does splinter, which is possible, these projections are off and Trump will not win. Ultimately however, the Republican elites' objections are likely just part of them coming to grips with reality. The majority of the globalists will ultimately stay – both for the sake of their own image and believability and because they will not want to see Hillary Clinton, much less Bernie Sanders, make Supreme Court nominations.

Though they may be globalists against Trump's brand of 21st century

Jacksonian/Theodore Roosevelt nationalism, they must know that should they split the Republican Party, they will never win again. And people like to win.

***

Takeaway:

Always be consciously aware of the recency and primacy effects. Put out maximum effort to ensure a favorable or unforgettable first impression. Always end your interactions or sales pitches on a high note, one that is conspicuously higher than all the rest. When listing benefits, list the most enticing first and last.

Final Thoughts

American history and human history in general has a knack for producing the right kind of people to meet the challenges of the time and galvanize the public into action to solve them. This may just be coincidence, but I think it's more likely that certain people have a knack for recognizing vacuums, making a proper offer for that vacuum, and having the sales skills to see it through. This brings about a new era for the people – and for those leaders' own benefit and personal glory. If those key people didn't have those skills, they would soon be replaced by others who did. History may have a natural selection of sorts to it.

Whether you love Donald Trump or absolutely despise him, I hope that by reading *Stumped*, you've come to recognize his playbook. Far from being an unhinged, unstable lunatic, each move he makes is carefully calculated and tested to produce the best result.

Donald Trump has been a speculated presidential candidate for decades. Yet, now was the time he finally chose to run. Why? Because he saw the vacuum. He saw the uncertainty, the electorate in revolt. He knew the crowd was clamoring for someone to give it answers. In his groundbreaking campaign that has thrown out all the ivory tower's rules, Donald Trump has done just that. In doing so, he's revealed secrets about us as people that were open, yet masked. Trump has defied the entire establishment and imposed his will on reality. He hasn't taken orders from anyone else. He's eschewed long-established rules that he rightly understood were growing increasingly tiresome on the public.

Donald Trump continues his hard-fought, but seemingly unstoppable march to the magic number of 1,237 delegates to secure the Republican nomination. When he gets there, he'll have done so because of his adherence to the principles laid out in this book.

These principles are there for you to use as well. You can play by the established rules of the world and operate only on the narrow band of light called the visible, or operate in the entire spectrum of light – view the world in the way it really is, and act accordingly. Play by Trump rules and master your own reality. The

Republican establishment has finally come to grips with and seems to be slowly accepting Trump's candidacy because he forced them to. He amassed a movement behind him and took the winds in his own direction.

The principles laid herein will help you to do the same. Even if you despise Trump, learn from his game.

Donald Trump also has an ability that has not been discussed until now – the ability to fight like hell and keep fighting until he wins, allowing nothing to stand in his way.

Upon planning his Persian expedition, it was said that Alexander the Great visited the Oracle at Delphi to try to discern the will of fate and fortune, only to find that the Oracle was not currently providing services. He was told to come back at a later date. Not accepting this, Alexander attempted to drag the Oracle to the temple, upon which he was told – "you are invincible, my son!"

That was all Alexander needed to hear.

Later, when on campaign, he came across the Gordian Knot, the knot that was said to award mastery of the world to whoever untied it. Alexander, declaring that the fable did not specifically say how the knot needed to be undone, took his sword and cut it open, untying it that way.

Alexander didn't play by anyone else's rules, and neither does Donald Trump. Both would not accept defeat and fought until they won. Trump remarks in *Crippled America*:

> I'm not a diplomat who wants everybody else to be happy. I'm a practical businessman who has learned that when you believe in something, you never stop, you never quit, and if you get knocked down, you climb right back up and keep fighting until you win. That's been my strategy all my life, and I've been very successful at it.
>
> Winning matters. Being the best matters. I'm going to keep fighting for our country until our country is great again.[126]

Although Donald Trump's campaign is undoubtedly self-serving, I must now risk sounding overtly enthusiastic about him in the last pages of this book. I cannot help but admire how Trump, whether through a selfish desire for power, ardent patriotism, or likely both, quite frankly, has given hope to millions who did not have it before. People have been searching for a leader to turn the country around from what they saw as consistent, stifling failure, and Trump has answered that call thus far.

Something good may yet come out of Donald Trump's candidacy. He may just break, or rather help to break, the power of the plutocratic class that so many Americans are in revolt against and reinvigorate American democracy for the next generation. That's what realigning elections have often done.

All transitions have their share of controversy. Many can be ugly. The fear of the unknown is very much prevalent, which naturally causes people to lash out. Those distinct realigning elections – 1800, 1828, 1860, 1896, 1932, and 1968 were all particularly nasty and ugly.

At the end of this current bumpy transition, we may yet find something better.

I'm naturally the optimistic type, so I tend to look at the big things and trends realistically, but brightly if I can.

What I can be certain of is that if we study and apply the principles of marketing and influence that Trump is bringing to his campaign, principles which the average person or the ivory tower "expert" for that matter, does not understand, as seen by how baffled most have been by Trump's rise, we'll be better off in our own lives. That is the greatest opportunity that Trump provides to the man at the grassroots – not as a leader, but as a topic of study.

Notes

All citations have been done in the format style of the American Political Science Association.

Introduction: Defying Convention, Rethinking Assumptions

[1] Carpenter, J.M. 2015. "Has Donald Trump Run Out Of Gas?" *The Masculine Epic.* http://masculineepic.com/index.php/2015/10/03/has-donald-trump-run-out-of-gas/ (March 27, 2016).

[2] Adams, Scott. 2015. "Dilbert Creator Scott Adams On Donald Trump's Linguistic Kill Shots." *Reason TV.* https://www.youtube.com/watch?v=55nxkenplg4 (March 20, 2016).

YouTube video

Chapter 1: The Masculine Monster in the Beta Sea

[3] Louis XIV. Published 1806. *Memoirs Of Louis XIV.* London: Printed for Longman, Hurst, Rees, and Orme, Paternoster Row.

Harvard College Library, Gift of Mrs. E.D. Brandegee, November 9th, 1908

http://books.google.com/books?id=M2EUAAAAYAAJ&printsec=frontcover&source=gbs_ge_summary_r&cad=0#v=onepage&q&f=false

[4] Taleb, Nassim Nicholas. 2012. *Antifragile: Things That Gain from Disorder.* New York, NY: Random House.

[5] Bartholomew, James. 2015. "I Invented 'Virtue Signaling'. Now It's Taking over the World." *The Spectator.* http://www.spectator.co.uk/2015/10/i-invented-virtue-signalling-now-its-taking-over-the-world/ (March 20, 2016).

[6] See https://twitter.com/billkristol/status/623848295832666112

[7] Cernovich, Mike. 2015. "Masculinity Always Wins." *Danger & Play.* http://www.dangerandplay.com/2015/10/15/masculinity-always-wins/ (March 25, 2016).

[8] Greene, Robert. 1998. *The 48 Laws Of Power.* New York, NY: Viking Books.

[9] Veloso, Maria. 2013. *Web Copy That Sells.* 3rd ed. New York, NY: AMACOM.

[10] Louis XIV. 1806. *Memoirs Of Louis XIV*. London: Printed for Longman, Hurst, Rees, and Orme, Paternoster Row.

Harvard College Library, Gift of Mrs. E.D. Brandegee, November 9th, 1908

http://books.google.com/books?id=M2EUAAAAYAAJ&printsec=frontcover&source=gbs_ge_summary_r&cad=0#v=onepage&q&f=false

[11] Cernovich, Mike. 2015. *Gorilla Mindset*. Middletown, DE: Mike Cernovich.

Chapter 2: Dominate that Space!

[12] Cernovich, Mike. 2015. "Masculinity Always Wins." *Danger & Play*. http://www.dangerandplay.com/2015/10/15/masculinity-always-wins/ (March 25, 2016).

[13] Veloso, Maria. 2013. *Web Copy That Sells*. 3rd ed. New York, NY: AMACOM.

[14] Trump, Donald J. 1987. *The Art Of the Deal*. New York, NY: Ballantine Books.

[15] Trump, Donald J. 1987. *The Art Of the Deal*. New York, NY: Ballantine Books.

[16] Trump, Donald J. 2015. *Crippled America*. New York, NY: Threshold Editions.

[17] Pressfield, Steven. 2004. *The Virtues Of War*. New York, NY: Doubleday.

[18] Veloso, Maria. 2013. *Web Copy That Sells*. 3rd ed. New York, NY: AMACOM.

Chapter 3: Frame, Attack, Counterattack

[19] Pressfield, Steven. 2004. *The Virtues Of War*. New York, NY: Doubleday.

[20] Greene, Robert. 1998. *The 48 Laws Of Power*. New York, NY: Viking Books.

[21] Adams, Scott. 2015. "Dilbert Creator Scott Adams On Donald Trump's Linguistic Kill Shots." *Reason TV*. https://www.youtube.com/watch?v=55nxkenplg4 (March 20, 2016).

YouTube video

[22] Pressfield, Steven. 2004. *The Virtues Of War*. New York, NY: Doubleday.

[23] Navarro, Joe. 2006. *Read 'Em And Reap*. New York, NY: Harper Collins.

[24] Greene, Robert. 1998. *The 48 Laws Of Power*. New York, NY: Viking Books.

[25] Pressfield, Steven. 2004. *The Virtues Of War*. New York, NY: Doubleday.

[26] Greene, Robert. 1998. *The 48 Laws Of Power*. New York, NY: Viking Books.

[27] Adams, Scott. 2015. "Dilbert Creator Scott Adams On Donald Trump's Linguistic Kill Shots." *Reason TV*. https://www.youtube.com/watch?v=55nxkenplg4 (March 20, 2016).

[28] Greene, Robert. 1998. *The 48 Laws Of Power*. New York, NY: Viking Books.

[29] Navarro, Joe. 2006. *Read 'Em And Reap*. New York, NY: Harper Collins.

Chapter 4: Politics or Pro Wrestling?

[30] Greene, Robert. 1998. *The 48 Laws Of Power*. New York, NY: Viking Books.

[31]   Oppenheimer,   Mark.   2008.   "Charm   School."   *The   Boston   Globe*. https://www.boston.com/bostonglobe/ideas/articles/2008/07/20/charm_school/?page= full (March 20, 2016).

Quoting Joseph Roach

[32] Adams, Scott. 2015. "Dilbert Creator Scott Adams On Donald Trump's Linguistic Kill Shots." *Reason TV*. https://www.youtube.com/watch?v=55nxkenplg4 (March 20, 2016).

YouTube video

[33] Trump, Donald J. 2015. *Crippled America*. New York, NY: Threshold Editions.

[34] Navarro, Joe. 2006. *Read 'Em And Reap*. New York, NY: Harper Collins.

[35] Court, Emma. 2016. "Donald Trump Is the Low-Stress Candidate, Voice Analysis Finds." *MarketWatch*. http://www.marketwatch.com/story/donald-trump-is-the-low-stress-candidate-voice-analysis-finds-2016-01-15 (March 21, 2016).

[36] Greene, Robert. 1998. *The 48 Laws Of Power*. New York, NY: Viking Books.

[37] Wiseman, Richard. 2012. "Self Help: Try Positive Action, Not Positive Thinking." *The Guardian*. https://www.theguardian.com/science/2012/jun/30/self-help-positive-thinking (March 21, 2016).

[38]   Cernovich,   Mike.   2014.   "Charisma   And   Connection."   *Danger   &   Play*. http://www.dangerandplay.com/2014/06/01/how-to-build-charisma-connection/ (March 21, 2016).

Mike Cernovich Podcast

[39] Greene, Robert. 1998. *The 48 Laws Of Power*. New York, NY: Viking Books.

Chapter 5: The Crowd Shrink

[40] Greene, Robert. 1998. *The 48 Laws Of Power*. New York, NY: Viking Books.

[41] Veloso, Maria. 2013. *Web Copy That Sells*. 3rd ed. New York, NY: AMACOM.

[42] See Robert Cialdini's *Influence: The Psychology of Persuasion*.

[43] Copyblogger. 2014. *Email Marketing*. Copyblogger Media.

Ebook

[44] "8 Social Psychology Experiments: Revealing Insights Into Our Behavior." 2012. *Psyblog*. http://www.spring.org.uk/2012/03/how-society-works-8-revealing-psychological-insights-into-our-social-behaviour.php (March 21, 2016).

[45] Oppenheimer, Mark. 2008. "Charm School." *The Boston Globe*. https://www.boston.com/bostonglobe/ideas/articles/2008/07/20/charm_school/?page=full (March 20, 2016).

[46] Silver, Nate. 2016. "How We're Forecasting The Primaries* *And Why We Might Be Totally Wrong." *Five Thirty Eight*. http://fivethirtyeight.com/features/how-we-are-forecasting-the-2016-presidential-primary-election/ (March 21, 2016).

[47] Neyfakh, Leon. 2016. "Nate Silver Said Donald Trump Had No Shot. Where Did He Go Wrong?" *Slate*. http://www.slate.com/articles/news_and_politics/politics/2016/01/nate_silver_said_donald_trump_had_no_shot_where_did_he_go_wrong.html (March 21, 2016).

[48] Reynolds, Glenn Harlan. 2016. "Glenn Reynolds: A Trump Wave Is on the Way." *USA Today*. http://www.usatoday.com/story/opinion/2016/02/25/donald-trump-supporters-brexit-preference-falsfication-2016-primaries-column/80856410/ (March 24, 2016).

[49] Veloso, Maria. 2013. *Web Copy That Sells*. 3rd ed. New York, NY: AMACOM.

[50] Copyblogger. 2013. *How to Create Content that Converts*. Copyblogger Media.

Chapter 6: Making it Personal

[51] Trump, Donald J. 2015. *Crippled America*. New York, NY: Threshold Editions.

[52] Cernovich, Mike. 2015. *Gorilla Mindset*. Middletown, DE: Mike Cernovich.

[53] Campbell, Margaret C., and Kevin Lane Keller. 2003. "292   2003 By JOURNAL OF CONSUMER RESEARCH, Inc. ● Vol . 3 0 ● September 2003 All Rights Reserved. 0093-

5301/2004/3002-0010$10.00 Brand Familiarity and Advertising Repetition Effects." *Journal of Consumer Research* 30: 1–13. http://vivaldipartners.com/pdf/brandfamiliarity.pdf (March 24, 2016).

[54] Campbell, Margaret C., and Kevin Lane Keller. 2003. "292   2003 By JOURNAL OF CONSUMER RESEARCH, Inc. ● Vol . 3 0 ● September 2003 All Rights Reserved. 0093-5301/2004/3002-0010$10.00 Brand Familiarity and Advertising Repetition Effects." *Journal of Consumer Research* 30: 1–13. http://vivaldipartners.com/pdf/brandfamiliarity.pdf (March 24, 2016).

[55] Veloso, Maria. 2013. *Web Copy That Sells*. 3rd ed. New York, NY: AMACOM.

[56] Greene, Robert. 1998. *The 48 Laws Of Power*. New York, NY: Viking Books.

Chapter 7: The Popular Revolt of 2016

[57] Malone, Adrian, Carl Sagan, and Ann Druyan. 1989. *Cosmos: A Personal Voyage*. United States: Cosmos Studios.

Cosmos Home Video Release

Chapter 8: Someone Make Me an Offer!

[58] Trump, Donald J. 1987. *The Art Of the Deal*. New York, NY: Ballantine Books.

[59] Dougherty, Michael Brendan. 2016. "How An Obscure Adviser to Pat Buchanan Predicted the Wild Trump Campaign in 1996." *The Week*. http://theweek.com/articles/599577/how-obscure-adviser-pat-buchanan-predicted-wild-trump-campaign-1996 (March 22, 2016).

Chapter 9: The Pendulum will Swing

[60] Trump, Donald J. 2015. *Crippled America*. New York, NY: Threshold Editions.

Chapter 10: The Don of Uncertainty

[61] Trump, Donald J. 1987. *The Art Of the Deal*. New York, NY: Ballantine Books.

[62] Trump, Donald J. 2015. *Crippled America*. New York, NY: Threshold Editions.

Chapter 11: The Realigning Election of 2016

[63] Washington, George. 1796. "Farewell Address."

[64] Abramson, Bruce, and Jeff Ballabon. 2015. "Trump Isn't the Real GOP Frontrunner." *CNBC*. http://www.cnbc.com/2015/12/23/trump-isnt-the-real-gop-front-runner-commentary.html (March 22, 2016).

[65] "Who's Really Voting for Trump: Portraits beyond the Polls." 2016. *Yahoo Politics*. http://news.yahoo.com/who-s-really-voting-for-trump---portraits-beyond-the-polls-061622809.html?soc_src=mediacontentstory&soc_trk=tw# (March 27, 2016).

[66] Howard, Ron. 2016. "Hillary Clinton Vs. Donald Trump — A Tough Battle." *Mercury Analytics*. http://www.mercuryanalytics.com/hillary-clinton-vs-trump-a-tough-battle/ (March 22, 2016).

[67] "Report: 46,000 P.A. Democrats Become Republicans Due To Trump." 2016. *CBS Pittsburgh*. http://pittsburgh.cbslocal.com/2016/03/10/report-46000-pa-democrats-become-republicans-due-to-trump/#.vug8buug1qs.twitter (March 22, 2016).

[68] Campanile, Carl. 2016. "Black Dems Aren't Turning out for Hillary like They Did for Obama." *The New York Post*. http://nypost.com/2016/03/18/black-dems-arent-turning-out-for-hillary-like-they-did-for-obama/ (March 24, 2016).

[69] Kutner, Max. 2016. "Armed With Chalk, Trump Supporters Are a New Breed Of College Republicans." *Newsweek*. http://www.newsweek.com/students-trump-old-row-chalkening-445923 (April 9, 2016).

[70] "The Common Sense Trump Coalition – A Post Election Night Debrief With Florida As a Predictive Microcosm…." 2016. *The Last Refuge*. http://theconservativetreehouse.com/2016/03/16/the-common-sense-trump-coalition-a-post-election-night-debrief-with-florida-as-a-predictive-microcosm (March 24, 2016).

Chapter 12: Piecing it All Together

[71] Hughes, Ken, ed. "Richard Nixon: Campaigns And Elections." *Miller Center*. http://millercenter.org/president/biography/nixon-campaigns-and-elections (March 25, 2016).

[72] Humphrey, Hubert H. 1976. *The Education Of a Public Man: My Life and Politics*. Garden City, NY: Doubleday.

https://books.google.com/books?id=L6u94c-7wX8C&printsec=frontcover&dq=The Education of a Public Man&client=firefox-a#v=onepage&q&f=false

[73] Safire, William. 1991. "Another `October Surprise,` In 1968." *The Chicago Tribune*. http://articles.chicagotribune.com/1991-05-26/news/9102160986_1_lbj-nixon-supporter-election-day (March 25, 2016).

[74] Bartlett, David, and Christopher Spencer. 2016. *Race For the White House: Nixon vs. JFK.* United States: CNN.

[75] Haffner, Craig, and Donna E. Lusitana. 2005. *The Presidents: Truman To Ford1945-1977.* United States: The History Channel.

[76] Leuchtenburg, William E., ed. "Franklin D. Roosevelt: Campaigns And Elections." *Miller Center.* http://millercenter.org/president/biography/fdroosevelt-campaigns-and-elections (March 25, 2016).

[77] Leuchtenburg, William E., ed. "Franklin D. Roosevelt: Campaigns And Elections." *Miller Center.* http://millercenter.org/president/biography/fdroosevelt-campaigns-and-elections (March 25, 2016).

[78] Leuchtenburg, William E., ed. "Franklin D. Roosevelt: Campaigns And Elections." *Miller Center.* http://millercenter.org/president/biography/fdroosevelt-campaigns-and-elections (March 25, 2016).

[79] Slayton, Robert A. 2011. "When a Catholic Terrified The Heartland." *The New York Times.* http://campaignstops.blogs.nytimes.com/2011/12/10/when-a-Catholic-terrified-the-heartland/?_r=0 (March 25, 2016).

[80] Craig, Douglas. 2002. "What Price Warren Harding?" *Humanities and Social Sciences Online.* http://www.h-net.org/reviews/showrev.php?id=6903 (March 25, 2016).

[81] Trani, Eugene, ed. "Warren G. Harding: Campaigns And Elections." *Miller Center.* http://millercenter.org/president/biography/harding-campaigns-and-elections (March 25, 2016).

[82] Craig, Douglas. 2002. "What Price Warren Harding?" *Humanities and Social Sciences Online.* http://www.h-net.org/reviews/showrev.php?id=6903 (March 25, 2016).

[83] "1904: Roosevelt v. Parker." *HarpWeek Elections.* http://elections.harpweek.com/1904/overview-1904-3.htm (March 25, 2016).

[84] "1900: McKinley v. Bryan." *HarpWeek Elections.* http://elections.harpweek.com/1900/Overview-1900-1.htm (March 25, 2016).

[85] "1900: McKinley v. Bryan." *HarpWeek Elections.* http://elections.harpweek.com/1900/Overview-1900-3.htm (March 25, 2016).

[86] "1896: McKinley v. Bryan." *HarpWeek Elections.* http://elections.harpweek.com/1896/overview-1896-1.htm (March 25, 2016).

[87] "1896: McKinley v. Bryan." *HarpWeek* *Elections*. http://elections.harpweek.com/1896/Overview-1896-3.htm (March 25, 2016).

[88] "1896: McKinley v. Bryan." *HarpWeek* *Elections*. http://elections.harpweek.com/1896/Overview-1896-4.htm (March 25, 2016).

[89] Haffner, Craig, and Donna E. Lusitana. 2005. *The Presidents: Cleveland To Taft 1885-1913*. United States: The History Channel.

[90] "1892: Cleveland v. Harrison v. Weaver." *HarpWeek* *Elections*. http://elections.harpweek.com/1892/overview-1892-4.htm (March 23, 2016).

[91] Ackerman, S.J. 1998. "The Vote That Failed." *Smithsonian Magazine*. http://www.smithsonianmag.com/history/the-vote-that-failed-159427766/?no-ist (March 25, 2016).

[92] "1888: Harrison v. Cleveland" *HarpWeek* *Elections*. http://elections.harpweek.com/1888/Overview-1888-3.htm (March 25, 2016).

[93] "1884: Cleveland v. Blaine" *HarpWeek* *Elections*. http://elections.harpweek.com/1884/Overview-1884-2.htm (March 25, 2016).

[94] "1884: Cleveland v. Blaine" *HarpWeek* *Elections*. http://elections.harpweek.com/1884/Overview-1884-3.htm (March 25, 2016).

[95] "1884: Cleveland v. Blaine" *HarpWeek* *Elections*. http://elections.harpweek.com/1884/Overview-1884-4.htm (March 25, 2016).

[96] "1880: Garfield v. Hancock" *HarpWeek* *Elections* http://elections.harpweek.com/1880/Overview-1880-3.htm (March 25, 2016).

[97] "1876: Hayes v. Tilden" *HarpWeek* *Elections* http://elections.harpweek.com/1876/Overview-1876-1.htm (March 25, 2016).

[98] "1876: Hayes v. Tilden" *HarpWeek* *Elections* http://elections.harpweek.com/1876/Overview-1876-2.htm (March 25, 2016).

[99] "1864: Lincoln v. McClellan" *HarpWeek* *Elections* http://elections.harpweek.com/1864/Overview-1864-2.htm (March 25, 2016).

[100] Holzer, Harold. 2016. "'Honest Abe' Lincoln Wasn't above Savvy Politics." *CNN*. http://www.cnn.com/2016/03/10/opinions/holzer-lincoln-douglas-debates/index.html (March 26, 2016).

[101] Bartlett, David, and Christopher Spencer. 2016. *Race For the White House: Lincoln vs. Douglas.* United States: CNN.

[102] "1860: Lincoln v. Douglas v. Breckinridge v. Bell" *HarpWeek Elections* http://elections.harpweek.com/1860/Overview-1860-2.htm (March 25, 2016).

[103] Cooper, William, ed. "James Buchanan: Campaign And Elections." *Miller Center.* http://millercenter.org/president/biography/buchanan-campaigns-and-elections (March 26, 2016).

[104] "James K. Polk: Campaigns And Elections." *Miller Center.* http://millercenter.org/president/biography/polk-campaigns-and-elections (March 26, 2016).

[105] Haffner, Craig, and Donna E. Lusitana. 2005. *The Presidents: John Q. Adams To Polk 1825-1849.* United States: The History Channel.

[106] Freehling, William, ed. "William Harrison: Campaigns And Elections." *Miller Center.* http://millercenter.org/president/biography/harrison-campaigns-and-elections (March 26, 2016).

[107] Sillbey, Joel. "Martin Van Buren: Campaigns And Elections." *Miller Center.* http://millercenter.org/president/biography/vanburen-campaigns-and-elections (March 26, 2016).

[108] Haffner, Craig, and Donna E. Lusitana. 2005. *The Presidents: John Q. Adams To Polk 1825-1849.* United States: The History Channel.

[109] Saunders, Andrew. 2016. "The First Time Party Bigwigs Tried To Stop a Front-Runner From Becoming President It Backfired - Big-Time." *Politico.* http://www.politico.com/magazine/story/2016/03/gop-2016-andrew-jackson-1824-213726 (March 23, 2016).

[110] Greene, Robert. 1998. *The 48 Laws Of Power.* New York, NY: Viking Books.

[111] Bartlett, David, and Christopher Spencer. 2016. *Race For the White House: Andrew Jackson vs. John Quincy Adams.* United States: CNN.

[112] Jefferson, Thomas. 1825. "From Thomas Jefferson To William Branch Giles, 26 December 1825."

From the National Archives' Founders Online http://founders.archives.gov/documents/Jefferson/98-01-02-5771 (March 26, 2015)

[113] Haffner, Craig, and Donna E. Lusitana. 2005. *The Presidents: John Q. Adams To Polk 1825-1849*. United States: The History Channel.

[114] Haffner, Craig, and Donna E. Lusitana. 2005. *The Presidents: John Q. Adams To Polk 1825-1849*. United States: The History Channel.

[115] Jefferson, Thomas. 1825. "From Thomas Jefferson To William Branch Giles, 26 December 1825."

From the National Archives' Founders Online http://founders.archives.gov/documents/Jefferson/98-01-02-5771 (March 26, 2015)

[116] Goodman, Bonnie K. "1816." *Presidential Campaigns & Elections Reference.* https://presidentialcampaignselectionsreference.wordpress.com/overviews/19th-century/1816-overview/ (March 27, 2016).

[117] Mieczkowski, Yanek. 2001. *The Routledge Historical Atlas Of Presidential Elections*. New York, NY: Routledge.

[118] Mieczkowski, Yanek. 2001. *The Routledge Historical Atlas Of Presidential Elections*. New York, NY: Routledge.

[119] Taylor, James C., ed. "John Adams: Campaigns And Elections." *Miller Center.* http://millercenter.org/president/biography/adams-campaigns-and-elections (March 25, 2016).

[120] Mieczkowski, Yanek. 2001. *The Routledge Historical Atlas Of Presidential Elections*. New York, NY: Routledge.

[121] Smiley, Tavis. 2004. "Thomas Jefferson, The 'Negro President'." *NPR.* http://www.npr.org/templates/story/story.php?storyid=1678026 (March 23, 2016).

[122] Taylor, James C., ed. "John Adams: Campaigns And Elections." *Miller Center.* http://millercenter.org/president/biography/adams-campaigns-and-elections (March 25, 2016).

[123] "The Common Sense Trump Coalition – A Post Election Night Debrief With Florida As a Predictive Microcosm...." 2016. *The Last Refuge.* http://theconservativetreehouse.com/2016/03/16/the-common-sense-trump-coalition-a-post-election-night-debrief-with-florida-as-a-predictive-microcosm (March 24, 2016).

[124] Adams, Scott. 2016. "Let's Talk About Hitler." *Scott Adams' Blog.* http://blog.dilbert.com/post/140800778006/lets-talk-about-hitler (March 23, 2016).

[125] Campbell, Margaret C., and Kevin Lane Keller. 2003. "292   2003 By JOURNAL OF CONSUMER RESEARCH, Inc. ● Vol . 3 0 ● September 2003 All Rights Reserved. 0093-5301/2004/3002-0010$10.00 Brand Familiarity and Advertising Repetition Effects." *Journal of Consumer Research* 30: 1–13. http://vivaldipartners.com/pdf/brandfamiliarity.pdf (March 24, 2016).

Final Thoughts:

[126] Trump, Donald J. 2015. *Crippled America*. New York, NY: Threshold Editions.

Index

ABOUT THE AUTHOR

J.M. Carpenter is a writer and entrepreneur who has worked on and off in New York politics since 2005. His background includes service with elected officials, working on campaigns, and experience in the non-profit sector. He received his B.A. in political science from Fordham University.

His websites, outskirtsbattledomewiki.com and masculineepic.com, receive over 30,000 unique visitors every month. You can follow him on twitter at: https://twitter.com/Duke_Libertas